MY 100 YEARS

In the Rhythm
& Flow

by
Jerri Brillhart

First published by Interdimensional Press

August 2017

ISBN: 9780991197040

Library of Congress Control Number: 2017947351

Printed in the United States of America

La Vergne, Tennessee

This book is printed on acid-free paper.

Dedication

This book is dedicated to the many friends and relatives who encouraged me to dream of publishing this book in my 100th year.

Acknowledgments

My thanks to my daughter, Suzanne Brillhart, whose careful eye and editing skills helped polish this book; my grandson, John Lund, who designed the front and back covers; my friend, Ginny Burns, who helped me edit and produce this book; and my publisher friends, Pat and Byron McCulley of Interdimensional Press, Brentwood, California. I especially want to thank Dr. Walter M. Bortz, who inspired me to live to 100 so many years ago. If it weren't for him, I wouldn't have had the dream to live this long!

Jerri Brillhart

Contents

List of Photographs

Foreword

It is a statistical fact that there are more people over 100 living today in the United States than ever before. It may startle people to know that living past 100 is natural, and that an even longer lifetime can be expected. In fact, our biogenetic maximum life span is 120 years. None of the organs decline with age as previously assumed. All the usual hallmarks of aging -- arteriosclerosis, kidney failure, and heart disease -- have been false prophets. Doctors must stop "medicalizing" the natural changes of aging.

In my book, "Dare to Be 100," I list 100 steps to 100, among them -- good nutrition, exercise, and rest are absolutes. Don't slow down. Don't depend on anyone else for your well-being. We all need to maintain mastery, autonomy, and independence in our daily lives. We have to see ourselves in our mind's eye as vital and alert and continuing to be interested in all the changes around us, and find an active part or role to pursue to find satisfaction. Accept challenges that force you to be alive and as creative as possible. We must continue to learn and grow mentally, and listen to our intuition as to how to continue to be happy for the rest of our lives.

About 40 years ago, Jerri Brillhart read an article I wrote and set out on her path to 100. Today, I'm pleased to celebrate the publication of her (first) book on this auspicious occasion.
She is living proof that we can all live to 100 and still be active, creative, and healthy individuals sharing this wonderful journey called Life.

I look at life as a fountain of energy. Jerri's fountain is a gift to us all. I thank her for allowing us to shower in her energies.

Walter M. Bortz, M.D.
Professor of Medicine
Stanford University School of Medicine

Introduction

"Shall we have a goal to live to 100?" This question intrigued Geraldine "Jerri" Brillhart 38 years ago when she was a mere 62 years old She had just read an article by Dr. Walter M. Bortz II, one of America's leading scientific experts on aging. Jerri was inspired by his ideas and applied them to her life.

Back then, she wondered what it would feel like to reach the 100 year mark: "If I'm still walking, dancing, and exercising every day, I will say, 'Okay, let's give it a try. But I want to have all my faculties at 100. It has been done by many people, why not me?'"

Today, at 99, she is an active, vibrant, creative woman who inspires everyone she meets. She swims, works out at her local gym, plays bridge three times a week, and drives her own car. Recently she bought a new iPad, which she uses to send messages to family and friends. She even has a Facebook page, which helps her connect with new people and organizations.

So here is her story, in her own words. Like everyone else, she's had her ups and downs. Her life has seen its share of tragedies and challenges, not unlike your own. But through it all, she managed to rise above it, and keep her eye on the goal. And that goal was to live to 100 and still be an active, creative, and enthusiastic human being.

Jerri has always wanted to publish a book of poetry and reflections on life. I am honored to have helped her bring this dream to fruition. We all look forward to seeing her celebrate the publication of this book on her 100th birthday.

Ginny Burns

Always Flowing

We are always flowing,
Through time and space,
Creating unique experiences
With our minds and hearts;
Our beliefs and attitudes
Manifest positive or negative
Experiences from within.
So choose today to believe only
In peace, love and prosperity,
Flowing through you
Here and now.

The Early Years

Our early beginnings contain the seeds of our character. Digging around in the ashes of my past, it seems to me that the lessons I learned as a child were incorporated into my life in very subtle ways.

When I was born on September 23, 1917, there was a famous opera singer named Geraldine Farrar. By naming me "Geraldine" perhaps my mother hoped I would become a great singer. However, I had absolutely no talent in that direction. My father did have a beautiful voice as a young man but never aspired to develop it. Since "Geralds" and "Geraldines" often grow up to become "Gerries," I chose to spell my name "Jerri," a more feminine version.

My mother, Rose Black, was born in Chicago in 1893. She had very little formal education. She quit school at age fourteen because she did not like the way her teacher spoke to her. She went to work as an errand girl, delivering hats for a milliner, then later had a job as a switchboard operator for the telephone company. She married my father, James E. Patterson, at the age of twenty-one.

My father was a carpenter by trade, but was not well. For many years, he suffered from arthritis of the spine. He could work only for a short while, and often got laid off due to the harsh winter conditions in Chicago, which halted outside projects. Then too, his health was precarious, which added to the uncertainty of steady employment.

My mother became the main financial provider for our family. She worked hard to take care of us. While employed by the telephone company, she decided to start a Hosiery Club. Silk hosiery was a popular item for women in the 1920s. But at $5.00 a pair, they were too expensive for the average working woman to afford. In the Hosiery Club, a woman was issued a small card with numbers on it. Each week, my mother collected twenty-five cents from each member and punched their card to record their payment. After twenty weeks, the cards would show a value of $5.00 and could be redeemed for hosiery. Who wouldn't jump at the chance of spending twenty-five cents a week for silk hosiery?

Even while working the night shift, my mother continued to manage this ever-growing Hosiery Club. Word spread and customers kept multiplying. Soon, she outgrew the small closet in her bedroom that was piled high with hosiery boxes. In 1922, she decided to rent a store on Roscoe Street near Riverview Park and, in addition to silk hosiery, sold lingerie, house dresses, scarves, gloves, and beaded jewelry. One might say she was a self-made businesswoman, listening to herself and following her own advice.

I was about five years old when we moved into the back of the store on Roscoe Street. Our apartment consisted of a large main room, which was a combination living room, dining room and kitchen with a sink and ice box in the corner. There was no couch or soft chair to sit on, only a round walnut table and straight-back chairs in the kitchen. There were two bedrooms, one for my sister and me, and one for my parents. There was no real bathtub, only a porcelain sink on a pedestal. You pulled a chain to flush the toilet, which had a wooden water tank at the top. In the cold of winter, we shoveled coal into the potbelly stove. On Saturday night, my mother heated water on the stove so we could take our weekly bath in a round metal tub. There was only one window that looked out onto the building next door. There was no backyard for us to play in. But we could play inside if we were quiet so as not to disturb my mother's customers.

A door in the kitchen led to the store and this was the only way in and out of the apartment. There was always a state of confusion in my household because tending to the customer was my mother's primary concern. People were always streaming in and out with their stories of pain or pleasure, and she was dispensing whatever item was necessary, whether it was hosiery or just reassurances that everything in their life would turn out okay.

I did not realize how different my home was from other homes. My mother's business was our life. There was constant movement flowing from the store to the kitchen. When the door to the store opened, a bell sounded and my mother would immediately leave the kitchen table at meal times to serve the customer.

My mother ran a kind of three-ring circus, trying to serve and please her customers, and also take care of her family. But for us, there was very little beauty, color, or sunshine in the somber surroundings behind the store. The only excitement came when new merchandise arrived. There were new dresses to look at, silk underwear and stockings in small cardboard boxes that were placed on the shelves. Fancy colored beads were sold in small glass tubes. Greeting cards were arranged on racks. Ladies gloves, handbags and handkerchiefs were displayed in the glass showcase.

I spent most of my time in the rear of the store when I was not attending school. Since my sister was too young to be left alone, I was appointed her caretaker while my mother tended to her customers. We were expected to be quiet. We played with our toys or games and were not allowed to be in the front of the store when the customers were there. Having other children play in our rooms was not allowed, since my mother could not handle additional children and still serve her customers.

One day when my mother was entertaining some neighbors, I came into the living room carrying my sister, and my mother got upset because she thought I would drop her. It was then that I imagined I was a mother taking care of my baby. At a very tender age, little did I know, I was to become a second mother to my sister.

While we were always well fed and well clothed, a certain kind of attention and nurturing was missing in our home. One of the most vivid, traumatic childhood memories was the time I played doctor with my sister while my mother was busy with a customer. I told my sister to lie down between the two dining room chairs and fall asleep. Then, I would give her something nice to smell when she woke up.

I found a bottle of liquid under the kitchen sink with a label showing a cute little girl in a pretty blue dress and a bonnet with blue ribbons holding a shepherd's staff. Of course, I could not read well enough to understand the words "Little Bo-Peep Ammonia" and "POISON" on the label. I took the bottle and opened it. When my sister raised her head up, I poured the liquid into her mouth and she immediately choked and started to scream.

My mother came running back to find out what had happened. When she discovered what I had done, she said, "I'll kill you! I'll kill you if anything happens to your sister!"

My sister's tongue was swollen for three days while I waited in terror. I thought my mother would surely kill me if she died. But, fortunately, my sister recovered without any serious injury. From then on, I feared my mother more than I loved her. It took me years to recover from that traumatic experience. I have since forgiven my mother, but it has taken a long time to do so.

Forgiveness

When I say "I forgive"
It is an act of love
A way of giving up my error
A way of giving up my criticism
A way of giving up my ignorance
A way of giving up my attitude.
As I empty all of my debris,
Suddenly I am free to allow
My heart to open up
To receive the light and
I am ready to change and grow,
Allowing the transformation
Of my feelings and my thinking
So that I am able to receive
An act of love...
A way of accepting all the truth
A way of accepting all the beauty
A way of accepting all the wisdom
A way of accepting all the blessings
And I am filled with thanks and joy
That keeps overflowing and broadcasting
Happy vibrations in my surrounding world.

My Word

Perhaps words, while being our mental tools,
Can sometimes be used for destruction
Without thought or care.
Words can be lethal weapons that escape
Our lips before we can retrieve them.
Such words sear our memories for a lifetime.
They can be so potent that their
Vicious effect can be seen in
Distorted lives that are filled
With discord, pain and misery.
Words that carry the power of love
Into manifestation for all to see
Are the precious tools we can use
To bring beauty, joy and happiness
To everyone we meet.

Center Stage

My mother was strong in determination,
High in enthusiasm, but short on patience.
She could see through the smoke screens
Of people's problems and excuses.
She was a woman of action and persistence,
Sharp of tongue and strong on humor.
She called a spade a spade.
She was a mover and shaker,
Always on center stage, even at 86.
Am I exhibiting these same traits
Even though I cannot see inside my heart?
I can only surmise
That it has often been said
The apple does not fall far from the tree.
Upon scrutinizing my own offspring
I can sometimes see
Traces of my mother's personality
Coming into view through
Little bits of behavior,
Attitudes and quirks,
That makes me raise my eyebrows
Heavenward, calling on my mother
With a fervent prayer:
Please help them
On their center stage!

The Little Shop
On Roscoe Street

Looking back, I know my mother did the best she could, considering the times and her limited education. She worked hard to take care of her family. She was often impatient and scattered, but also resourceful, creative, and above all, hopeful. Her intuition ran at high gear and most of the time she was right on target. She laughed at my fears and pushed me out into the world to take risks and find my way. She taught me in subtle ways how to have patience and strive to understand the people I met. She was curious about all people and was always trying to figure out what she could sell them to make a profit.

Throughout the 1920s, my mother's little shop on Roscoe Street flourished. When I came home from school, there were dresses in the showcase and thin boxes of expensive silk hosiery wrapped in tissue paper piled up on the shelves. Those were the days when children were seen but not heard, and my sister and I were confined to the back rooms, where we played quietly with our toys.

I could hear the clang of the cash register, which I was forbidden to touch. The streetcar ran down the middle of our street on a trolley and periodically its clatter would fill the air. You could hear the noise from blocks away. It was a necessary conveyance, and by the age of six, I learned to use it along with a transfer when I went alone to the Southside of Chicago to visit my grandparents. For me, it was a means of freedom to explore the sights, smells, and sensations of Chicago.

Roscoe Street served as a good example of how enterprising people made their living in the 1920s. It was lined on either side by a variety of stores, and most of them had living quarters in the rear or above where the merchants lived with their families. It was a predominantly German neighborhood. My mother fit right into the community since her mother, Teresa Bender, had immigrated from Germany to seek a better life in America. A tiny woman, Grandmother Teresa married a man 10 years her junior, which was unusual for the time.

Near my mother's shop was a German delicatessen and bakery that had fresh rolls piled high in the window every morning. The grocery store had barrels of pickles floating in brine, and a glass case filled with penny candies and enticing cookies. My favorite was a chocolate covered marshmallow with a pecan on top. A few doors down from my mother's shop was a silent movie theater where I spent most Saturday and Sunday afternoons with my sister watching Tom Mix serials and the "Perils of Pauline." The movies were a safe place for my sister and I to go since my mother was busy on Saturdays selling her merchandise. On Sundays, my parents sent us to the matinees so they could have a few hours of quiet time for themselves.

In the summer, an ice cream cart came by and sometimes we were treated to a vanilla cone. There was also another small vehicle that drove up and down the street selling freshly made waffles sprinkled with powdered sugar. I also remember seeing the organ grinder with a trained monkey dressed in a red coat and cap. The organ grinder played some lively music while the monkey cavorted around to amuse the crowd. Every time a person dropped money into the monkey's hand, he would take his hat off in thanks.

One of the highlights of the summer was waiting for the iceman to deliver large blocks of ice. He would take his icepick and cut the huge blocks to the size and weight requested by the customer. The iceman sometimes gave us small chipped pieces to suck on if we were watching him cut the ice. It was so refreshing to suck on those cold pieces on a hot summer day! In the winter, the same company delivered coal to the basement for the stoves and furnaces.

At the age of seven, I learned how to sew and do embroidery. I embroidered a dress with French knots and by the time it was finished it was too small for me so I gave it to my sister. I was so proficient at sewing, I even helped my sewing teacher. I loved to sew clothes for the Kewpie doll I kept in a shoebox. My mother called me "busy fingers" because I was always making something, spending hours by myself cutting and sewing.

So what did I want to be when I grew up? I certainly didn't want to be tied down to a business for six days a week working like a Trojan, buying and selling, and having so much excitement all the time. I thought it might be fun to be a clothing designer. At 13, I won a prize in a sewing contest sponsored by a Chicago department store. I made myself a three-piece wool suit consisting of a skirt, jacket and short cape. The prize was a certificate for yardage in the sponsoring store. With the material I won, I made a summer dress.

My mother opened her first store in 1922 when I was five years old. In 1926, she moved to a larger store located at 2024 Roscoe Street. We lived in a small, rented apartment nearby. Her business flourished and was listed on Dun and Bradstreet, which made her feel important. To reduce costs and supplement her stock, she often bought items at auction. In 1929, she went to an auction sale where she suspected that the merchandise had been stolen. She took her suspicions to a nearby Chicago police station.

One Sunday morning, she went to the store to prepare for the week ahead. She unlocked the front door and was shocked to discover that all her stock was gone. She had been robbed during the night!

On that bright, full moon night in June of 1929, a group of men drove up in a big truck, jimmied open the front door of the store, and stole most of my mother's merchandise of hosiery, lingerie, house dresses, scarves, gloves and handkerchiefs, thereby stealing my family's livelihood.

Later, a neighbor living across the street in a second story apartment told my mother that she watched a large van arrive after midnight, and people began moving everything out. She thought it was my father and some of his friends unloading the store, so she never called the police.

Because my mother didn't have any insurance to cover her losses, she was forced to declare bankruptcy. We survived by the generosity of family and friends. That summer we moved to Hot Springs, Arkansas, so that my father could take the cure for his arthritis. In the fall, we moved back to the Southside of Chicago and rented an apartment where we could finally eat all our meals together like every other family, without being interrupted by customers needing attention.

When I entered Parker Junior High School in the Fall of 1929, my mother went to work selling practical, everyday merchandise from our car, driving to homes so she could meet her customers in person. She continued to go to auctions to buy merchandise.

My father's parents were well off financially, and helped us through the Depression. My grandfather, John L. Patterson, came from Toronto, Canada and was a fine cabinetmaker, and a 32-degree Mason. They owned their own home and a Rickenbacker sedan.

I admired my grandmother for the lovely home she kept, the delicious meals she served, her formal table settings and spiritual knowledge based on the Christian Science religion. She was a very impressive, artistic and intelligent woman for her day. I remember she wore such beautiful hats and had manicured hands. In many ways, she was a major influence in my life. She paid special attention to me in a way that my mother never did.

Family holidays were celebrated at my grandparents' large home since we never had room for guests in our small apartment. The most pleasant memories of my childhood centered around these family gatherings. My father had two sisters and one brother and it was an exciting time to be able to play with my three girl cousins. The big event was watching my grandfather carve the turkey on Thanksgiving Day. The smells of those holiday dinners at my grandparents' home will remain with me always. Years later, I remember having holiday dinners for my own family and I was unconsciously following the same pattern of creating a festive dinner that my grandmother had created years ago. This is how traditions are transferred from generation to generation.

One event stands out in my memory. When I was about ten years old, my cousin Roberta and I decided to "kidnap" the turkey carcass a couple of hours after it had been carved up and consumed by the family. Everyone was still sitting around the living room visiting, while Roberta and I quietly sneaked into the kitchen and took the entire roasting pan containing the remains of the turkey.

We crept upstairs to the bathroom, where we had a wonderful time picking the turkey bones behind the closed door. I supposed the stolen food was much sweeter than the food eaten under the scrutiny of our elders, because we were doing such a forbidden thing. I cannot recall if we were caught in the act or whether we returned the turkey-roasting pan to the kitchen before we were discovered. It was such a strange thing to do; I have never forgotten it to this day.

During the Depression, my grandmother bought our family warm clothes for the winter. I was often invited to stay a few weeks at their home during the summer. She would take me shopping in downtown Chicago, known as the Loop. When I graduated from high school, she gave me a beautiful sapphire ring that I cherish to this day. Often I would look at this ring and be reminded of the first time I saw it and remember my grandmother's words, "Look at how it shines!" It has remained a shining memory of her love and the many moments we shared when I was young. She had been a guiding light throughout those difficult years. Her love sustained me and the memories I cherish of her were far more valuable than the sapphire ring she bought for a song during the Depression.

When I was a teenager my father told me I wasn't as good looking as my mother. I really needed to hear that from my father! We did have our differences, and not much love was lost between us. But I did learn to forgive him because he was in so much pain that he taught me how to be sympathetic. I also learned how important it was to take care of my body and stay healthy.

It is said that we choose our parents before we incarnate so that we can learn lessons from them that help strengthen our souls during our earthly journey. I certainly learned many lessons from my parents. From my mother, I learned perseverance and to make the best of everything. She taught me how to be strong and self-reliant, for which I thank her to this day.

In my teenage years, however, I often felt both of my parents were unreasonable and unsympathetic. I would often daydream about running away, but where would I go? Sometimes I fantasized that someone would come and take me to another place and I secretly thought of what clothes I would take if I had to leave in a hurry. I wanted to grow up faster so I could leave.

Remembering

As I hold a picture of my 16-year-old self
I meditate long and weary over what I see.
There was very little joy in that unloved soul,
An accumulation of worn-out attitudes that
Caused my heart to be as heavy as their own.
Childhood is often a struggle for existence
To hold on to God's eternal joy.

The Depression Years

It was 1934 and the middle of the Great Depression. I was seventeen when I met my first boyfriend, Rollin, who was two years older than I. We were introduced by mutual friends, Ione and Ed, who belonged to the same Methodist Church I attended. During that summer we double-dated, and Rollin and I became fast friends.

After graduating from Parker High School, I attended Moser Business College, studying Gregg shorthand, bookkeeping and typing. After completing the nine-month course, I could take shorthand at 100 words per minute and type 60 words a minute. I was ready to find a job.

But finding a job in the Depression was a bit tricky since work was scarce and every business wanted someone with experience. My first opportunity came about because my grandfather had a close friend who was personnel director for a large insurance brokerage firm called Marsh & McLennan. After reviewing my qualifications, Mr. Padgett hired me at a salary of $75 a month. In those days, there were no fringe benefits, just a two-week vacation after completing one year of service.

At 18, I was the only one in my family with a steady income. My grandmother Martha co-signed a line of credit at the department store so I could buy myself a fine winter coat. When I forgot one of the payments, she called and said, "I know, Geraldine, you will take care of this." This taught me a great lesson and I never missed a payment again in my life. It is from such backgrounds that a strength of independence and responsibility for oneself flourishes.

Raised during the Great Depression in Chicago impressed upon me the necessity of making the best out of life. I heard many tales of illness and woe. I learned from others that life was hard. To grow up in that world took courage, strength, and faith that everything would eventually change.

Survivors of those Depression years tell stories about their determination to succeed despite all the obstacles. Those who had the desire to overcome their circumstances worked hard to make their dreams come true. Somehow they learned that optimism and positive thinking created a happy, successful life. Negative thoughts created by their own ignorance had to be overcome as they followed their passion. Some people learned the art of visualization, which simply means the ability to hold a vision of what you wish to accomplish. However, even with academic or material success, one should also strive to achieve wisdom and understanding in order to find lasting peace and happiness.

At Marsh & McLennan, I worked in the Records Department, recording pertinent information on large, heavyweight cards. I used a very heavy, oversized typewriter, which slid back and forth across my desk. The large sheets of paper were placed under the typewriter and the keys came down on the flat surface of the paper. It was a cumbersome contraption and difficult to move. Although I was not able to use my shorthand skills, I was happy to be working and gaining experience in the insurance business, which would be a valuable asset in the future.

Three months later, my father was diagnosed with tuberculosis and sent to a sanitarium in San Fernando, California. My mother and sister followed him four months later.

After working a year at Marsh & McLennan, I took my two-week vacation and boarded a train for California, arriving in Los Angeles several days later. Within one week, the Massachusetts Bonding and Insurance Company hired me. I immediately sent a Western Union telegram to Mr. Padgett telling him that I would not be returning to my job in Chicago.

When I moved to California in 1936, Rollin kept sending me special delivery letters every day. We missed each other, so he decided to take his vacation at Christmas to come and see me. He came by train and stayed with my mother and me in our furnished apartment in Glendale. At the time, my father was still in the sanitarium in San Fernando. After two weeks, Rollin insisted he could not find work in Southern California, and decided to return to Chicago. Later, he married a friend of mine, so that was the end of our relationship.

After my father was released as an "arrested tuberculosis patient," I moved into a boarding house in the Wilshire area of Los Angeles. It was a miracle that none of us caught tuberculosis from him while he was sick. My father and mother eventually moved to Cathedral City near Palm Springs.

Being nineteen years old and already having insurance experience under my belt opened some employment doors for me, and soon I found a real secretarial job in a branch office of a New York firm called Associated Aviation Underwriters. I remained in that position for the next five years.

When I was twenty years old, an extraordinary thing happened to me on my return from a church retreat in the San Bernardino Mountains. It was the winter of 1937 and the roads had been cleared of ice and snow, or so we thought. Ozzie, a young man from church, didn't have much experience driving the Pierce-Arrow convertible, but he seemed so sure of himself that he had already taken off the tire chains at the last rest stop.

As the car sped around a curve, I looked down the side of the mountain and into the gulley below. Chills went down my spine as I thought, "*What if we drive off the cliff and die?*" I tried to put those fears out of my mind and concentrate on the road ahead. Suddenly, the tires hit a slick patch of black ice and the car began sliding towards the gravel at the side of the road. Before we knew it, the car lurched forward and sideways, the canvas top ripped open, and we were both thrown out on opposite sides of the car.

I must have blacked out, because I never saw the car going end-over-end down the cliff, landing 350 feet below in a smoldering pile of metal.

I awoke to find strangers standing over me. "Hey, Miss! You sure are lucky to be alive. If you hadn't been ejected from the car, you'd be dead as a doornail!"

Fortunately, we weren't seriously injured, although Ozzie had a dislocated shoulder. Later, as I lay in the hospital bed recovering from a few scrapes and bruises, it occurred to me that what I had feared had come true. Somehow my thoughts had either contributed to or predicted the events that took place. But I also knew that God had spared me. It was truly a miracle.

When I returned to Los Angeles, I began attending lectures by Ernest Holmes and Neville Goddard, learning about Science of Mind principles and the power of the mind to control one's experiences. These powerful ideas helped me navigate through the many ups and downs of my life for years to come.

A New Life

The most adventurous twelve months of my life occurred between June 1940 and June 1941. I was almost 23 years old and still working as a secretary for Associated Aviation Underwriters in the Bartlett building at Seventh and Spring Streets in Los Angeles. I decided to take my two-week vacation in mid-June. I told my landlady at the boarding house that if she had a chance to rent my room while I was away, she could move my belongings into the dormitory with two other girls.

On the longest day of the year, I found myself on my first cruise on the *S.S. Alaska* enjoying the midnight sun. It was my first long vacation alone and I had high hopes of meeting the young man of my dreams. I shared a very tiny cabin with an 80-year-old woman who was going to Skagway to live. I took the upper berth going to Skagway, and had the cabin all to myself coming back.

After my vacation, I returned to my boarding house, where I met a new boarder named Bill Mattson. He had moved into the bedroom I had vacated. I had unknowingly prepared a place for the love of my life!

We dated that summer, driving everywhere in his new 1940 Oldsmobile. He had driven it all the way from Washington, D.C. where he had been trained to work in the newly established Social Security Administration.

In September of 1940, Associated Aviation Underwriters sent me to Chicago for about three months to help set up a branch office. It was my first flight and I was a little frightened but still willing to do it. It was an overnight flight on TWA out of Burbank. At that time, airplanes had sleeping berths on night flights and I remember using the little white paper bag during the flight. After arriving in Chicago the next morning, I checked into the elegant Stevens Hotel on Michigan Avenue.

After a few days there, I arranged to live with the McGuire family on the Southside where I had lived before I left Chicago. They were like my second family. Their daughter, Ione, was my best friend and I used her room since she was away at college.

While in Chicago, I visited my grandparents, and other friends, so all in all it was a lot of fun. When it came time for me to return to California just before Thanksgiving, the Home Office arranged for me to fly to New York to visit headquarters and meet the people who worked there. I stayed at the Waldorf Astoria while they showed me all the sites.

Taking the return flight from New York to Los Angeles in 1940 was a long, tedious, up and down event that involved refueling and picking up new passengers. Bill Mattson picked me up at the airport and we began talking about a future together. One evening a few days later, he drove me up to the Observatory in Griffith Park. As we looked out at the city lights below, he took out a black velvet box from his coat pocket, and presented me with a diamond engagement ring from Donovan & Seamans.

On the first day of winter in 1940, at ten o'clock in the morning, I married William Gustav Mattson in a simple, ten-minute ceremony performed in "The Niche" of the First Congregational Church in Los Angeles. Bill and I wore navy blue suits and I had an orchid on my left shoulder. My mother, sister, and Charlotte and Eugene Graves were the only witnesses present. We had not even discussed the possibility of a large formal wedding. There was very little money to spend on frivolous things, and too many relatives and friends lived out of state.

After the quick ceremony and the well wishes of those present, we drove to Riverside, California, stopping at the famous Mission Inn for a champagne luncheon. We both felt a bit self-conscious in our new roles of Mr. and Mrs. Mattson.

We drove to Palm Springs for our honeymoon and spent our first week in a little bungalow beside the swimming pool - - a true Hollywood setting. Palm Springs was just a small resort town consisting of about two blocks of stores and motels. We danced at the El Mirador Hotel on Christmas Eve and I felt like a movie star in my long white gown.

We took long drives around the area, explored Salton Sea and the Indian reservation. Later, we drove to Sacramento where we spent New Year's Eve at the Senator Hotel and dined and danced with the Flannigans. Bill had made friends with them while being trained in Washington, D.C.

In those days, a woman was expected to be a virgin on her wedding night. Women worked hard to maintain that status until they got married. Perhaps the fear of unwanted pregnancy was more the reason for remaining chaste until the wedding night.

I can recall as a teenager wanting to read books about sex to gain information, and discovered that all sexual books in the library were in a locked case. I was too embarrassed to ask for those kinds of books, so I just believed, like most women, that nature and my husband would teach me what I needed to know.

Looking back on those years, I realize how different life was. Today, instead of having sex information locked up in libraries, the reverse has occurred. Sex is a subject discussed in newspapers, radio, TV and the Internet. The sanctity and privacy of what goes on behind closed doors is now material for open discussion.

Back in the 1940s, life was slower, saner, and more dignified. The newspapers, magazines and radio programs stressed the ethics and values of a good family life. Men were encouraged to love, honor, protect and provide a wholesome environment, while women were called "homemakers." People in the 1940s lived mostly within their means. There were no credit cards to tempt

31

them into living in a fantasy.

Upon returning to Los Angeles, we moved into a furnished one-bedroom apartment on Grandview Avenue. I started to cook and clean and get on with my new life and my new name. A few months later, I learned to my great surprise that I was pregnant.

We didn't have much money back then, so I thought it would be nice if we could "demonstrate" some more money, especially now that I was pregnant. This was a prosperity technique I learned in Science of Mind programs offered by Ernest Holmes.

Holmes wrote: "Every time you say, 'I am a little short of funds,' 'I haven't as much money as I need,' you are putting a limit on the substance in your own consciousness. Is that wisdom? You want a larger supply, not a limited supply of substance. Therefore it is important to watch your thoughts so that the larger supply may come through your mind and into your affairs. Say to yourself, 'I am God's offspring, and I must think as God thinks. Therefore I cannot think of any lack or limitation.' It is impossible that in this universal Mind that fills everything there can be any such thing as absence. There is no lack of anything anywhere in reality. The only lack is the fear of lack in the mind of man. We do not need to overcome any lack, but we must overcome the fear of lack."

"Let's see if we can demonstrate $10,000," I said to my husband. He said okay, fine, he'd go along with that.

"What would you do with $10,000 if you had it?" I asked.

He laughed. "Well, I'd give it to you, of course!"

Little did I know, five years later I would receive $10,000 from my husband, but not the way I expected.

On Mother's Day in May 1941, we bought our first home in the Mar Vista area of Los Angeles. Fritz Burns was the developer and this was his first attempt at building affordable housing on a large scale. Our home on Military Avenue near Palms cost about $4,800 with $500 down. It was a typical house with two bedrooms, one bath and a one-car garage. We moved in July and had fun planting grass and buying furniture. That same month I left Associated Aviation Underwriters, having worked there for five years.

Our daughter was born on November 12, 1941, and immediately captured my heart. I named her Marsha after the popular movie actress Marsha Hunt, but she never developed into an actress. She started playing the violin at the age of seven, and to this day she entertains both young and old with her music.

Less than a month later on December 7, 1941, Pearl Harbor was attacked and life immediately changed for all of us. To avoid being drafted into the service, Bill went to work for the defense contractor McDonnell Douglas in the Accounting Department. We had to adapt to wartime regulations, like nightly blackouts and ration stamps. We were all doing our duty to win the war.

Two years later my second daughter was born. I named her Marilyn, mainly because I wanted both my daughters to have the same initials. I was a stay-at-home mom for the next few years. I learned to grow green beans and can fruits and vegetables with a pressure cooker. But for reasons I will never understand, I had a nagging fear that my husband would die and leave me all alone. Maybe it was the war that brought these negative thoughts and fears upon me, or maybe it was something else, a sense of foreboding I could not shake.

I tried to push my fears down and go on with my life, but in November 1945, Bill became quite ill. He was hospitalized and eventually diagnosed with polio. Within one week he had died, leaving me to raise our two young daughters alone.

Departure

In the morning stillness
I hear and remember you
When our lips first touched
In the beginning of our intimacy
And kindled the warmth within me
To blend with you.
Our breath mingled
And the flow of hearts
Began to comprehend
That our spirits were again
United to carry forth
An uncompleted dream we shared
In the mysteries of another time.
At first our lives flowed joyously
But then our paths became divided and
You made your departure to the unseen shore,
While I wept with self-pity,
Seeking reasons for your quick demise
Until I came to understand
That change must occur
So we each can grow
In new directions
Of divine fulfillment.

Blue Heart

Once my heavy blue heart
Was filled with sorrow that
Spilled over in tears and pain,
Stretched by anguish and change.
Blindly I carried on in spite
Of my numbness and closed mind.
Slowly with time and necessity
Something inside me began to grow.
My tears stopped flowing,
My heart started to mend,
And then it blossomed
Into a new beginning.

His, Mine & Ours

During the following year, I tried to pull myself together. I left the Baptist Church because of too much pity from friends. I started attending Unity Church, where many of the Science of Mind principles were being practiced. I had to find a new way of living, a more positive way of thinking.

Unbeknownst to me, Bill's employer, McDonnell Douglas, provided a life insurance policy of $10,000. When I realized this was the exact amount of money we had asked for at the start of our marriage, I was shocked and saddened. I couldn't help but feel guilty about taking that $10,000. I would have never asked for that money if I had known it would come to me through the tragic death of my husband.

After he died, I was very careful of what I wished for. Nevertheless, it was just enough money for me to manage the next chapter of my life as a single mom. Since housing was scarce at that time, I used some of the insurance money to buy a house with extra bedrooms, and opened up my home to seven young ladies who rented sleeping rooms. It was the best of both worlds, since I was able to stay at home with my daughters and earn a living at the same time.

It was through one of these ladies that I met my second husband, George Brillhart. It was in the summer of 1947 that I had a vacancy in my rooming house. Since I did not want to advertise in the newspaper, I called Robinson's Department store in downtown Los Angeles and explained what I had available to rent. They told me they would send a representative to inspect my home and then post a notice on their bulletin board.

Soon Peggy called and arranged to come and take a look. She subsequently moved in with the help of a nice looking man. Peggy was friendly and fit right in with the other six girls. One evening in

October a few of us were having a discussion in the living room when suddenly Peggy said, "I know just the man for you, Jerri. He is too old for me but he would be just right for you."

Much to my surprise she immediately went to the phone to call him and said, "George, would you like to take my landlady out to dinner?" He told her he would call me back later. To make a long story short, we went out to dinner the next Saturday night.

George and his first wife were divorced in 1940 when his daughters were 10, 11 and 12. He was awarded custody and had been raising them alone. We continued dating and discovered we were very compatible and loved each other, despite our 17 year age difference. All my women roomers moved out in January and George and I were married in Unity Church on January 27, 1948.

We took a three-week honeymoon, boarding the *S. S. Corsair IV* in San Pedro. This sailing ship accommodated 85 passengers and had previously been owned by J.P. Morgan as a private luxury yacht. It took two weeks to cruise to Acapulco, Mexico where a private English-speaking guide picked us up. Over the next week he drove us to Taxco, Cuernavaca, Mexico City and Vera Cruz, making all the necessary hotel arrangements and showing us the sites. Those were memories I cherished for many years.

While we were away, George's two youngest daughters moved into my house, where my sister, Shirlee, was taking care of my daughters. Rita, his first daughter, was already married with two children. Lois, his second daughter, was married six months later so that left Dana, the youngest, who was with us for two years. It felt odd to be a step-grandmother at the age of 30. Over the years, I felt more like a sister to my three stepdaughters than an actual stepmother. George and I then added to this mix with our own child. Susan, who later changed her name to Suzanne, was born one day before our first wedding anniversary in 1949. We now had his, mine and ours to produce a very special blended family.

In 1952, we moved into a newly planned suburban town near Los Angeles called Lakewood. Our daughters attended newly built schools from elementary through high school. Throughout the 1950s, I became active in the school's PTA, and eventually served as its President.

But I was not satisfied with motherhood alone. I was seeking some kind of spiritual fulfillment, apart from my husband and children. Ever since my grandmother introduced me to the Christian Science religion, I was drawn to people who believed in positive thinking, healing, and metaphysics. Fortunately, there was a Science of Mind church near my home. There, I met people who shared many of my own deepest beliefs and I immediately felt at home. It was the beginning of a long journey of spiritual growth and personal fulfillment. In 1956, I received a practitioner's license in the Science of Mind Church of Long Beach.

Three years later, I found myself going back to the ranks of the employed, beginning a 21-year career with Travelers Insurance Company in Long Beach. After I retired in 1980, I decided to further my education. I joined about 40 other retirees in a group known as Continuing Learning Experience (CLE) later OLLI (Osher Lifelong Learning Institute) at California State University, Fullerton (CSUF). I traveled all over the world with people from this organization, fulfilling my lifelong desire to travel and expand my horizons.

Journeys

I have always been obsessed with a desire to travel. I remember sitting in my high school study hall, daydreaming about what I would rather be doing than reading textbooks. I fantasized that someone would come one day and take me away. Was there a deeper reason for wanting to leave and go to some far-off place?

When I was young, my curiosity about other people and parts of the world was very intense. I had a burning desire to learn and know. I wanted to see these places first-hand, rather than read about them in books. The desire to see and feel and hear sounds of distant countries claimed my attention.

My first travel experience was by train, when I left Chicago to move to Los Angeles. At age twenty-three, after three years of working at Associated Aviation Underwriters, I finally had my first opportunity to do some real traveling. Jumping on the train to Seattle, I joined a cruise to Alaska, shortly before I married Bill Mattson and started having children.

With marriage and family duties to fulfill, I didn't get another opportunity to travel until 1966, when I took my mother on a flight to Hawaii. This was when I caught the "travel bug" and started making yearly trips with friends, since my husband George didn't like to travel. I made two cruises to Alaska, one in 1940 and another in 1978. I cruised to Mexico in 1948 and 1978. That year, I also cruised to the Caribbean, San Blas Islands and the Panama Canal. In 1970, I went to Japan, Thailand, the Philippines and Hong Kong - - all for a remarkable price of $1,195 including hotel, meals, and airfare. My first trip to Tahiti was in 1971, and I went back in 1974 and 1981.

After I retired in 1980, I was free to explore the world even more. As a member of the Continuing Learning Experience group from 1980 to 2009, I took classes in writing poetry, bridge, watercolor painting, history, computers, etc. I also took many overseas trips with this group, including trips to Europe in 1983, China in 1985, England and Scotland in 1989, Canada in 1993, Turkey in 1994, Calgary, Banff and Jasper in 1999, and Spain in 2000. I have also been to Caracas, Venezuela. My doctor told me in 2016 I could live another 10 years. I am ready!

The Journey

Usually, when you start a journey, you prepare yourself. You plan what you will take, how long you will be away, and what you will do along the way.

As a rule, we think of a journey as a vacation or a trip having a beginning, middle, and end. Sometimes you are forced to move out of your home for one reason or another. Sometimes you may journey to a foreign land and start a new life.

Sometimes a journey is long and uneventful or filled with new sights, smells, and sensations. Sometimes a journey can be disastrous and filled with negative experiences.

We might say that a journey always teaches us something. It could be a process of expanding our perceptions and judgments.

Every journey begins with anticipation and desire for the unknown. Often we meet a new person who appeals to us. We take time to understand them when we take small journeys with them. Even going to dinner, a movie, a lecture, a picnic, or a dance, can be considered short journeys of exploration.

Each day we journey into our environment and recreate, reinvent, and reinvest our time to find new satisfactions in surviving another day in our journey on Earth.

Since we have been in the process of this Earthly journey all our lives, many of us have come to realize how we have trusted a Higher Power to sustain us, guide us, and prepare us for each experience, and will continue to do so even when our Earthly journey has come to an end.

My Spiritual Journey

At around seven years of age, I was introduced to Christian Science by my Grandmother Patterson. I often took the streetcar during the summer to spend weekends at her house. She took me to the Christian Science Sunday School, where I heard Bible stories about how Jesus healed people. Neither of my parents went to church, so my Biblical tales fell on deaf ears.

It was from such a beginning that I wondered about other churches, so when I was about ten years old, I went by myself to a Baptist church a block away from my house to listen to Bible stories. Again, I tried to tell my mother what I had learned in church, but she was too busy with her store to even listen or care.

When my family moved to an apartment on 72nd Street across from the Normal Park Methodist Church, I attended this church regularly and began to make friends. I enjoyed their friendships for many years. But I always wondered why they never told us or demonstrated anything about healing people like they did in the Christian Science church. My mind was full of questions, but it was many years before I found out more about faith and how it is practiced. I began my spiritual journey at this point.

When I moved to Los Angeles in 1936, I attended Sunday morning lectures by Ernest Holmes, who had written a book called "The Science of Mind." He would say over and over, "There is a power in you that will work for you if you will release it."

I was now at the point where I could use my imagination for good and my life opened up as I began to use these principles. After I married Bill Mattson in December 1940 and started to have children, I wanted our girls to be raised and taught religious principles. Bill and I were baptized in the Baptist Church on Easter Sunday in 1945. The war was coming to an end and we felt at last life would be better for everybody. However, tragedy struck in the fall of 1945, when my husband died of polio and I became a widow with two small children.

My spiritual journey took a new turn, helping me through my grief and pain toward a new way of thinking, and the knowledge that all experiences were a result of "divine right action."

Fallen Leaves

In my heart I discovered
Varied colored fallen leaves,
Telling me of my journeys.
Some are dark and some are light,
Old and preserved memories.
Some relived, energize me.
Each are my soul's legacy
Lying close, lingering near.
If some leaves in my life
Have caused me sadness,
I must learn the poignant lesson.
But if by chance I spy light ones
Gleaming in my earthly sojourn,
Let me retrieve the essence
Of those bright leaves to
Teach me if I find
I'm growing old.

Words & Writing

Before I could even read or write, words were etched into my brain by my mother, through nursery rhymes. I was her first born, so she had fun listening to my little voice repeat the words back to her. I suppose I was being conditioned by this experience to love words because they were somehow associated with the love she was pouring through them and my childish way of responding to her. The bond between us was being formed word-by-word, thought-by-thought.

In later years, she confessed to me that I was the only one she had ever truly loved. In some ways, that might have been a feeling she secretly held in her mind.

Be that as it may, I learned at a very tender age that words were important. Words could help you learn, and I developed a passion for books, and reading those words on the page satisfied my curiosity about the world around me.

In my early years, I heard my mother's words often repeated: "Children are to be seen and not heard." Because she said them often enough with such emphasis, she planted those words indelibly on my brain and no matter how old I became, my mother's words kept returning to my mind.

Another set of words that were handed to me were, "Good, better, best, never let it rest, until the good is better and the better best." Those words skipped along so precisely and neatly that they were like a chain around my neck. I got those ground into me so well, that to this day they keep nipping at my heels as I try to run away from them.

The best of all these words she taught me were, "This too shall pass." They kept me keeping on despite the challenges and problems I encountered in my life. These words were the survival tools I clung to over the years. In the depths of my being, they sustained me, and my use of them protected me in the dark passages of time.

When I joined a troop of Girl Scouts in 1925, little did I know that the words I learned to say each week would become buried in my subconscious mind and create values to live by. The Girl Scout motto was, "On my honor I will do my duty to God and my country, helping people every day, especially those at home." I realize that the simplicity of that motto kept me going through both the good times and the bad. The values embedded in my mind worked at a subconscious level and guided me. So I could truly say, those values never changed for me. The basic idea of duty to God, country, and family has given me a sense of balance and stability throughout my life.

* * *

The real problem with words is that there are so many of them running through my mind that I lose them before they can be captured in an article, story or poem. My world is colored and sprinkled with words. They mostly run around inside my head and I could spend hours amusing myself with words issuing from my imagination.

Words make me cry, they make me laugh, they make me sing, they make me love, they make me celebrate. They sometimes amuse me for hours and I have nothing to show for my time. I want to tell it like it is, or like it might be, or like it should be, or like I would like it to be. The words are alive inside of me, growing more profusely with time. I sometimes seem to be choking on them because they are bottled up inside of me and I don't find time to let them out.

In recent times I have been wondering why I am allowing these words to be dammed up instead of springing out like other people's words seem to be, cluttering up the atmosphere with descriptions of their trips to the doctor or their headaches; especially the older ones who are constantly giving me the "organ recital" of their recent operations.

Words sometimes get in the way of love, by the overuse of "shoulds" and "should haves," when kinder and more thoughtful words could have mended broken hearts.

Oh, yes, words can bring laughter, suspense, murder, violence, love or hate. They can be false or true words, imagined or real. They can communicate a feeling within the heart or just tell something about a smile. They can describe an event or sway an audience by the rise and fall of words with hidden meanings.

It seems to me that the network of civilization would crumble if suddenly the use of words was lost or forbidden. What mighty changes words can bring!

The only way to put all those words running around in my head to any earthly good is to express them in a positive way. They must be coaxed out with discipline and training. They must be written down and examined, and trained to behave in an orderly manner. While the child in me was told to be seen and not heard, I am trying to become the adult who has earned the right to be heard.

* * *

Writing has always been a dream of mine, my secret ambition. It's scary to pin down a wispy kind of feeling called a dream, isn't it?

When I was a teenager, I read short stories and novels and I often wondered if I could ever write original stories like that. I had no idea how people wrote the things I enjoyed. I only felt it would be fun to do it some day. I even made some feeble attempts at expressing myself over the years through letters, poems, and journals.

Perhaps I have been practicing writing all my life as a hobby. I really wish I had kept a diary from as far back as my teenage days when I first received a diary as a small gift. The few minutes a day it might have taken to capture my thoughts or experiences could have been fodder for a novel today. I was so busy with other things that I didn't discipline myself enough to write consistently.

Am I really just dreaming of being a writer or can I begin to really discipline myself at this late stage to sit at a typewriter or computer for a few hours a day? I know that would be the first real test of opening up and getting down to this business of writing.

Am I still dreaming instead of working? Dreams are pointers trying to get our attention. Rather like a still, small voice that nags us about what we should be doing, we make up a thousand excuses of why we don't have time to pursue our dreams.

* * *

I must start writing whatever is on my mind. It is a way of exercising the subconscious to get in the flow.

Days of routine keep me moving through the hours. When I am without a purpose or commitment, I seem to waste my time. The unproductive hours slip away. Of course, the earth sometimes must lie fallow before the next crop is planted, and that is how it seems as I am living in my ninth decade.

My energy is slacking off. I seem to be standing still. The flow of energy must be directed by desire and imagination or the well will run dry. When I stop planning or imagining, I stop the flow and begin to die. My spirit stops flowing outward and I am non-productive. In a way, I am preparing for my next incarnation.

I look at where I have been and what I have done with my life. There seems to be so much I have not learned or accomplished. However, I sense I always had some inner guidance that I used to keep myself moving in a certain direction. As I look back, I discern a pattern emerging that shows me what I really accomplished in my life.

Instinctively, the salmon returns to the stream where it was born when it is time to die. I believe human beings, in some manner, do the same thing. They return in consciousness to a certain void that was there when they were born. It is a kind of resignation to the natural scheme of things. It is an orderly way of adjusting to a new phase of being.

As babies are born from the void and emerge into life, they are fed and hopefully taken care of by loving people who are ready to teach them about their new life. It is the same when they move out of the human experience into the Infinite void that we call eternal life. The circle is complete as we return to the so-called void from which we sprang.

* * *

Writing is releasing ideas through thought and placing them on paper. Creative ideas come from within the inner life, the personal analysis of experiences that only you can tell. You should write your feelings. It is much like an artist using paint and brushes to place on canvas what she sees and feels. There is something the artist desires to share and express, and that expression presses out from her center.

Most of the time the creative artist acts like a channel, allowing the flow to occur. You come alive by creating, because you are allowing the source of yourself to come forth. This is why creative activity is a joy and a zest. It allows you to enjoy yourself, and satisfies you like nothing else.

Writing or any creative activity takes an act of will and desire. You literally will it to happen by placing yourself in the state of mind whereby you operate in a receptive attitude. You place yourself in a state of readiness or a kind of inner listening, believing that ideas will manifest.

Some writers have to wear a certain kind of clothing. Some have to work at a certain hour of the day. Some have to be alone. Some have to be in a public place. These idiosyncrasies are a kind of belief system that works for them, a trick or device that helps them set the mood or a kind of trance that overcomes anxiety or feelings of inadequacy.

Experiment with yourself as to when and where you are comfortable for creative endeavors. Every writer is unique in how he or she goes about producing. Sometimes a writer needs to be sparked by being with other writers because they interact and give and receive ideas from each other.

Whatever allows the juices to flow, go for it. Open up the right side of your brain and forget the logical left side. Be innovative and creative in your own unique way.

Words

We are filled with many words.
We are exposed to them everywhere.
They are on the Internet, TV and in books.
Some are beautiful or helpful.
Some are fearful, sad or hurtful.
Many are strong enough to break your heart.
Some words stay with us for a lifetime
While others are lost or thrown away.
Some never forget their mother's words.
We use prayers to heal ourselves or others
While all the time our mind pays attention
To very special words coming from the heart.

Snowflakes

As I conspire to inspire
Through my addiction to words
I feel the closeness of myself.
It is in this timeless space
While surrounded by thoughts
Of such immensity that they
Overwhelm my senses
With the enormous idea
That I am spending such a
Short time in this vastness
Called my Father's House,
That words melt like snowflakes
Falling silently within me.

In the Quiet of Their Room

In the quiet of their room,
Women use time
To write about events
Of the human condition,
Expressing their feelings
In images engraved on their hearts,
Recording cycles of life
Moving through time,
Weaving tapestries of living
In nature's constant cycles
Of sun, moon and earth;
Their pens syncopate
To the myriad changes
That keep them growing,
Expanding and balancing
In their quietness.

My Baby

I once had this amazing dream. It was full of symbols and ripe for introspection. I roused myself back from outer space and went to my desk to capture the details so I could analyze it.

In my dream, I see myself holding a very tiny, fully developed, newborn baby. The baby's eyes are closed and it is only about one-inch long. It is floating in a small plastic envelope full of water. My first reaction is, *how will I feed this baby and help it grow?* I am both perplexed, pleased and apprehensive about its welfare.

In the next sequence I am walking in a business district looking in shop windows. I have the tiny baby with me. I see a man inside a store and he seems to recognize me. He has a threatening look on his face and starts to reach up to grab some bricks to throw at me. I immediately start running across the street, but fall down and have to crawl on my hands and knees to reach the other side. I get myself up and run into the vestibule of a building, where I wait until its safe to leave.

Of course, these symbols are all about me and I shall try to shed some light on this. To me, the baby represents my creative life, my "brain child" or one might say, "the right side of the brain." It is not fully awake but it has possibilities because it is perfectly shaped and represents the seed within me that needs the right kind of nutrients to grow.

I am hiding this baby within me but all of a sudden my logical left brain threatens to destroy it by hurling bricks of negative thoughts, such as: *You are too old to have this brain child!* Or it may be insulting like: *At your age, you should forget about working so hard. Who needs more stories, more poetry, more novels? The world is full of words and what good does it do? Save yourself the*

61

aggravation of rejection. Just end your days being logical and forget this brain child.

Something inside me weighs these thoughts on a scale of experience. At this point, my logical left brain is hanging in the balance, while my creative right brain is experiencing a new sense of freedom and joy of expression, nudging me on to go for it! I am getting the message and it is so stimulating that I feel young and happy, and I know I can allow this brain child to lead me into the center of myself and bring me satisfaction.

Delivery

I am so full and pregnant with words.
I feel labor pains engulfing me
Trying to birth this mental child.
There is no real physical pain;
It is just a kind of turning
A word or idea into a resting place.
I keep rolling over and over
Trying to be comfortable while
Ideas keep kicking at the
Inside of my swollen womb.
I am full and ready to give birth,
Laboring over a form of expression
Until in desperation I find a
Pen and paper and make my delivery,
Allowing it to be born alone,
Kicking, crying and taking a risk!

Creative Maturity

It is surprising how my perceptions of myself have changed and altered over the years. Just by taking a mental inventory, I have become stronger in my convictions about who I am and where I have been and how much creative ability I have. I have discovered a part of myself that was sleeping, just waiting for me to make demands upon it.

At times, this awakening to my inner life is rather startling. It gives me mixed feelings of wonderment, sadness and gladness, all wrapped up together. So now that I have found my voice, my true expression, what am I going to do about it?

Perhaps it would be well to sit down and write down what I would really like to accomplish. Just let myself go and imagine just what I would like to have happen. Now if this is too wild and I don't want to appear an idiot, I don't have to write it down; I can just think about it. That way, nobody can call me a fool or laugh at me.

The idea is, if we have a secret desire to accomplish something, sooner or later the desire will express itself in our life experience. You are the creator of your life. That may surprise some of you because you probably thought that things just happen to you by chance. You are always creating your life by what you believe and think. The thought or belief always precedes the event in your life.

So let's work for ourselves and not against ourselves. If we say, "I am afraid I am not creative. I really can't write anything interesting," then that is what will happen, because you are not giving positive suggestions to yourself that you are creative.

So think about what you want to accomplish and give yourself lots of nurturing and loving care. Carry on an inner dialogue with this creative part of yourself and tell it things like: "*I am filled with creative ideas that I express easily every day.*" Or make up your own words that get you going.

Before you know it, you will be enjoying yourself immensely, living a very interesting and creative life!

Imagination

Stretching my imagination
Is much harder than stretching
My ancient rigid body,
Because the discipline of
Exercising physical mass
Is so very humdrum
That all the muscles
Just cooperate by
Repeated mindless movements.
But when I try to capture
Abstract wispy mental
Connections that can turn
A "nothing idea" into a
"Something thing"
It seems so utterly
Impossible to squeeze my
Imagination into a form of
Material substance that
When it happens
I am blown away!

The Greatest Gift

We all possess within our hearts
The gift of imagination.
As we discover and use it,
We find we can create
Our very own happiness, or
Bring ourselves unhappiness.
Every day we use our imagination
To enrich or destroy ourselves.
It is how we use our mind
To create joy, peace and love
To accent positive ideas with
The gift of our imagination.

Love

The wisdom of love sustains and transforms us. It benefits the giver as well as the receiver. To experience authentic love, we must come to that inner awareness of our need for love and its redeeming qualities.

When our pain and loneliness reach unbearable proportions, we are at the breaking point and reach out for help. It is like a man drowning and fighting for his life. At that point, we become acutely aware that we must move in a new direction.

No longer will the old alibis and excuses work. A new kind of truth-telling must come into awareness. We must risk the peril of dying to our old beliefs and dig into ourselves for better ways of living a more truthful and natural life in mind, body, and soul. As we let go of negative points of view, the fog lifts and we become free to express our own uniqueness. As we replace fear with faith, we grow in a new way. All anxiety is a form of fear:

F - False
E - Experience
A - Appearing
R - Real

We learn to tell the truth to ourselves about ourselves, without shame or blame. We become more authentic. We become more aware of our wants and feelings. We ask for what we need and we take the risk of believing our wants will be satisfied. We become co-creators, seeking to love ourselves as well as others, more abundantly. We join the human race in its struggle against the forces of evil. Remember, evil spelled backwards is "LIVE."

We accept the positive and create our own world by our belief about ourselves. We take responsibility at all times for the life we are living. This is not a problem; it is a challenge we must accept and move into a more balanced and happy life where we can make our dreams a reality. It is said that more than 97 percent of us come from dysfunctional families and we are suffering the consequences of this ignorance. We must awaken to these errors and learn better ways of communicating with each other.

Love

Love is the redeeming quality
Lifting our ebbing spirits,
Renewing body, mind and soul,
Giving us the invisible strength
To meet every change of life.
If we have erred in perception
Our body will reveal ignorance;
If we fail to find happiness
Love will give us guidance;
If we find ourselves in debt
Love will supply our abundance.
The invisible thread that holds us
In a state of wholeness and strength
Is the presence of love within us.
Love is the magic
And great mystery of life!

Expectations

Out of the wilderness we come
With our expectations and desires,
Hoping, praying, and wishing.
We try to believe that life
Will be better than all
Our follies of yesteryears,
Our risks, mistakes and failures
Suffered through trial and
Error while searching for
A brighter, saner, happier
Way of being, experiencing and
Ultimately dying to our old
Perceptions while still rising to
Greater and greater expectations.

Opening Up

How can love be withheld?
So many ways of closing ourselves off
From loved ones through indifference,
Selfish pursuits and pleasures
That build walls of isolation
Protecting us from imaginary rejection;
A game of hide and seek
So dramatically exhibited
In the act of love and intimacy,
Desiring the touch, the embrace
Satisfying flesh of the outer person
While holding back the inner spark
In fear that if the truth and
Total essence were given fully
Somehow our identity would be lost
Creating terror and anxiety to the Self.
So we hold back part of ourselves
Because of fear that if we trust and
Love completely and meet frustration
If we lost again, we would lose our
Sanity in grief once more.
So we cling too much to our independence
Protecting our Ego from this pain.
Can we overcome illusive comfort by
Restriction and mental constriction
Keeping us prisoners in this
Hell of our own contrivance?
Open up to your inner reality,
Let go of false beliefs,
Realize there is nothing
But the mind that fools us,
Holding us back from opening up
Our hearts and arms.

True Love?

We seek love because we need to have someone make us feel good. It gives us a warm feeling or "rush." We become addicted to the idea of needing that person for the love they give us and how they make us feel. We become their prisoner because we don't feel good about ourselves unless another person is touching us and giving us sexual pleasure. We like the feeling of love.

This kind of love based on sexual pleasure is not true love. We are needy for this pleasure of the body. We are satisfying an ego need and this kind of love is not true because it is subject to the whims of another person giving us this pleasure. If the other person withholds this body satisfaction there is unhappiness. There is hate. There is the unleashing of all the devils within the nature of the other person. There is mental and emotional cruelty inflicted in the so-called battle of the sexes.

Now, after a death or divorce, having lost this other person, to whom we had become a slave through this addiction, we usually seek a replacement to assure ourselves that we are a loveable and worthwhile human being. The new loved one substantiates this belief by showing us love and admiration. We are again trapped in this wonderful feeling of being in love and in loving someone else.

We are worshipping another person for our own need and ego pleasure. We are making the love object OUR GOD. This is why there is so much unhappiness, because when we worship another, we lose ourselves in that other person and we are not focusing on the reality of the spiritual God within us. This inner God-Self is always giving love and nurturing our needs and this is pure love without control or demands.

This type of spiritual love flowing through us must be contacted each day. A unity through meditation is the key to this complete realization of spiritual enlightenment. Then we do not need a church, a spouse, a car, a house, a certain power or social attainment to feed the ego. We have reached true love in the Promised Land of inner peace.

Love Lost

My marriage to George Brillhart lasted more than forty years. But as he approached his eighty-ninth year, he began to lose touch with life and I saw him slipping away from me. One day, I wrote down everything we said to each other, to show what it was like to lose somebody while they are still alive.

October 4, 1988

I am sitting upstairs with the fan on. It is 100 degrees and I am trying to keep cool. George comes upstairs and tells me that somebody is coming to take him home. He says this woman was downstairs today and now she is gone.

He is so confused. He doesn't know who I am. I tell him we have been married for 40 years, and he doesn't believe me. He looks at the twin beds in the bedroom and says, "How come if I am married to you, why don't we sleep together?"

I tell him he never wanted me to sleep in his bed. He wants to see the marriage license, to see if we are really married. He is lost.

He says he has been coming here regularly. He sees his clothes in the closet. Now he begins checking all the drawers for his clothes. He finds a box of checks and reads my name and his name printed on the checks. He can't quite figure it out. Now he asks if I have a car. He says he used to have a car but he lost his license. Two years ago he stopped driving. He says he doesn't care now. He says he has a bunch of clothes in the closet. I tell him this is his home. He says his brain is getting more settled . . . he used to be much more confused. He thinks his mind is getting better. He tries to be nice to everybody. He says he can remember everything.

He says the woman who lives here, that sleeps there, she put this clock here. I tell him I am Geraldine Brillhart, but he wants to see the mail with my name on it. He wants proof of who I am. So, I give him my driver's license. He now says, "I don't have any money . . . I don't work anymore." He wants to see the marriage license. Now he says, "Did I stay here last night? Do you have a car?"

Now he repeats that he can't drive anymore. Now he is muttering about his clothes again, as he looks through the dresser drawers. He asks, "Are you going to stay here? Are you running this place?" He says I am getting to look like someone he knows, but he wants to see the marriage license. I tell him it's in the safety deposit box and I will get it from the bank tomorrow. He comes over and kisses me and says it has been a long time since he touched a woman. Now he sees my bathing suit in the bathroom and he thinks it belongs to someone else. He thinks it belongs to "Geraldine." I tell him that is me. He now wants to look again at my driver's license to see if I am Geraldine. He shakes his head and mutters, "I come over here so often . . ."

Now he asks, "Where is your car?" I tell him "in the garage." He wants a ride. I tell him it is too hot. He agrees it is too hot. Now he talks about the clock on the dresser. The old one broke and a girl gave him that one. "The girl who sleeps in that other bed." Now he wants to know my name and I tell him and he still can't believe it. He wants to look again at my driver's license.

"I don't have any money," he says. "I don't know how much money I have."

He doesn't want me to pay all the bills. He says, "I am forgetful and I don't know what my income is. I get one check. I worked for one company and when I retired I got sixty-some dollars a month from them. I get Social Security and I don't know how much it is."

He shakes his head and says he doesn't keep a list. Now he looks in the checkbook box, looking for money. I ask him how much money does he have in his pocket? He counts $78 in cash. He says he has a little more in a savings bank. "It's not very much.

I don't get a helluva lot of money. But every month I get sixty-some dollars. The Social Security goes right to my bank. I don't know how much that is. I don't have any trouble otherwise."

He now asks, "Are you the only one here?" He is still confused about our being married. "How old did you say you are?"

"I am seventy."

"You are as old as I am."

"No, you are eighty-seven."

"We have to talk some more. Were you married before? Did you have children? Do you own this place? You could rent it out. Does your daughter live with you?"

"No," I say. "You live with me."

Now he wants to know if I own this place.

"Do you own other property?"

"Why would I want to own any more than one place?"

"Are you writing me a letter?" he asks, seeing me take notes as we talk. "The other girl who used to be here liked to swim."

"I am that girl," I say. "I am Geraldine."

"You mean, you and I are married?"

"Yes."

"Where did we get married?"

"Los Angeles."

"That's not in California."

"Yes, it is."

He says he's confused. He doesn't know where he lives. He keeps repeating this. Then he looks in the closet again to check his clothes out because I tell him he lives here.

"Something makes me come back here again," he says. "I like this place because I was here a couple of times. I kinda like the place, so that's why I keep coming back."

He starts to wander downstairs, and I follow.

"Do you want me to take care of you?" I ask.

"I don't know that I need so much care. I don't get mad or angry. I don't know where I live. I have to start walking to know where I live. I have all my clothes in there and upstairs."

"What do you want to do?"

"Well, I could come and live with you and try it out," he says.

Then he says he doesn't have any clothes. He doesn't know where to go to get his clothes. So then I tell him, "So, now let's just say you live here and just stay here."

"Well, yeah, then I will stay in the bed upstairs and you stay in the other bed."

"Well, that's settled then. You just stay with me."

"I don't have any relatives here and most of my sisters have died."

"Don't you have any children?" I ask.

"I think the first time I got married I had a couple of children. My first wife and children wanted to stay there and not come out West with me . . . I think I have pajamas upstairs in the right corner of the closet. I better go up and look; I don't want to sleep without my pajamas." He goes upstairs again, and I follow him into the bedroom. Now he asks, "What is your first name?"

"My name is Geraldine. Would you rather call me Jerri?"

"What is your right name?"

"It is Geraldine."

"My name is George F. Brillhart," he says, spelling it out for me.

He goes into the bathroom and sees his razor and other things. "I think I had a razor in the other place."

"Should I call anyone to tell them you are staying here?"

"I don't know too many across the way, or too many on this side."

Then he talks about the other people in the complex, including the man he thinks is an alcoholic. He says he has seen him walking and knows that his mother bought the unit and gave it to him. "I don't know how he cooks for himself. He is an oddball to me. He does his own laundry. He plays the piano . . . oh, yes, he was spoiled by his parents. I don't know where to find the house where my wife lives. She will probably call."

"Do you think your wife will be angry?

"I don't know, she is not very lovable because I tease her too much."

"Why do you do that?"

"The reason is I was the only boy and had four sisters. They were all older and they teased me."

"You didn't like it but you shut up about it?"

"Another fellow and I came to California when I was 25. I told my parents I was going to California. I got a job selling shoes. Worked in an office later. Totaling up figures . . . two brothers owned the company. They called it Wellington. Worked for them only six months. They didn't like what I did and I didn't like the way they treated me. Worked at another job doing figures. Then went back to selling shoes. Worked for Weatherby Kaiser, can't think of the other store. I like the city life. So much I have forgotten."

"Do you ever see your children?"

"I don't know, to tell you the truth. I got two or three. I don't like to jump around and move too much. What is your name again?"

"Jerri."

"The other girl's name was Jerri."

"You knew another one? Then it should be easy to remember. What do you like to do?"

"I like to walk, eat, sleep and do a little loving . . . but it don't work. It is hard to explain. I didn't ask the doctor."

"You can't get an erection? Does that make you uncomfortable?"

"Yes, it happened in this house, too."

"When did that happen?"

"It happened a year or a year and a half ago. I was ashamed in not responding to the sexual operation. I don't know what to say about that sexual thing. We could try it, but I don't know if it works or not. I don't know what to tell you about this thing. It doesn't work. If you don't believe me you can try it . . . "

We look at each other for a moment until his mind shifts again.

"You won't believe this but this morning I didn't know where I came from. I don't know where I lived. I could slit my throat because my brain doesn't work right. I don't know where I came from. I'll have to stay until I get something done to this crackernut. I wonder what I have at the other place I came from this morning?"

* * *

Duality

Dual personalities maneuver
In his rigid, fragile shell.
From his open sunny places
He plunges into chaotic spaces
Not knowing who he is or why.
There he is, the same old body
With an irrational, empty mind
That looks so strangely and
Begins to query me about
Why I came and if I live here,
Searching through my face,
Never recognizing me or our
Forty years together.
When his mind goes "click"
He sneaks out, leaving all
His life experiences
In a matter of a flash,
Losing all his rationality;
Every path of memory
Has vanished and there
He stands exposed in a
Different space of mind
Wandering in the same old body.

Simplicity

My husband always used to say
"Life should be simple."
His greatest expression was
"Keep it simple" or
"Just simplify."
His mind has lost
Some forty years
Of worldly accumulations and
He's simplified his life
By saying "I can't remember."

Changes

Hardening my heart against
The changes I observe
In your aging slumber,
Comparing what is
To what used to be,
Railing against your
Preparation for leaving,
Trying to cling too long
To that which is passing.
Instinctively you know
While trying to hold
The former shell in place
That one big quake will
Shake you off your pedestal
Into the next dimension.

Serving

I reach out to you
In your stoic silence
With my heavy heart,
Knowing that your wall
Is thick and dark,
Hiding you in a secret
Space where none can enter.
I knock in vain but
You never listen to the shouts
That lie muffled
In my throbbing throat.
I see your face, your smile,
Your familiar hands
Behind a wire mesh
While our time together
Has no meaning;
It is like sawdust
In my mouth, as I
Serve your daily needs.

Enduring Love

Holding you, saying
"I love you"
Is a total acceptance of all
Your endearing frailties,
Knowing how wondrous
You really are
Even when you forget
And your voice
Sounds angry and
Impetuous
Or your eyes glisten
With criticism
Those are the moments
That underneath you
Are so magnificent,
Recognizing all your
Values are honest and
Sincere, even when you
Can't remember
What I asked you
To do on Monday
Recalling all the years
Of gentle ways
You were when abandoned
To your amorous antics
That now lie dormant
On a secret shelf.
While love has mellowed
And been tamed to a tiny flicker.
I sit in service,
Still loving you.

To George

As you lie curled up
In that quiet spot
While the women walk by
Silently changing sheets
And dispensing tiny pills
To ease your agitation
And your pain
Dream away this reality
And ease into that place,
That other kind of space
Let the hours and days pass
As you shut out thoughts
Of other years,
Moving gently into the
Arms of Eternity.
Gently falls the rain
This March morn
Heralding another Spring
That will be born
Just as my tears
Fall in my sorrow
As you linger
In the shadows,
Waiting for the final breath
To take you home.
I shall sing when the
Sun shines and
The Spring blossoms
Showing its beauty,
Reminding me that
You have been
Reborn into an
Even greater glory.

Crucible

All that we have been
To each other is still intact.
Down under the layers of smiles
I wear as a mask, you are dried
Like clay, in the marrow of my bones,
Closer now than when you were alive.
I ache in my heart for our yesteryears
When you gladdened my life with
Those countless gestures, pats and
Strokes that made my heart sing in
Rhythm to your love and your anxieties.
Forty-one years of balancing our differences
In the struggles of life's crucible.

You

You are here today and gone tomorrow.
The spirit in you is the same spirit
That you had a thousand years ago.
You are the Beloved now and forever.
You are a one-of-a-kind reality
Using your body, mind and soul
To become more of yourself, connected
To and living within the same spirit,
Expressing through every living soul.
You are the Beloved
Manifesting as you.

88

Another Chance at Love

I was a widow in my 79th year when I thought I was not too old to dance again. So, I joined the Buttons and Bows Square Dance Group in Fullerton, California. I was having a go at my second childhood! Each week I learned a new call and how to swing my partner in the square. In June the next year I graduated with the beginners group. I bought new square dance clothes and was rejuvenated into a life of action.

I met Dick in the square dance group and he was also being rejuvenated by dancing. His wife had died and we became great buddies. He lived only five blocks from my house. At my 80th birthday party, I introduced him to my family as my "boyfriend."

Our relationship lasted 12 years. We traveled abroad. We played bridge and attended classes at California State University at Fullerton with the Continuing Learning Experience. We learned to write poetry and stories. We learned to use water colors and do abstract painting. We had a wonderful time together and I enjoyed those years and being a part of his family.

After his sudden death in March 2009, I moved to Northern California where my three daughters lived. I made new friends and opened new doors to a different life in Summerset II in Brentwood, California. I was 92 that year and on my way to creating a new chapter. Life was filled with many new possibilities!

Magic

The desire of my heart danced
Before my outstretched hand;
His smiles and expert grace
Captured my affection
As the square dance caller
Commanded us to doe-si-doe!
Week after week the bond
Increased with each step,
The music kept us twirling
To its insistent rhythm
Balancing our differences,
Until that magic moment when
We electrified each others' lips with kisses.

Enchantment

Your yearning eyes
Come flashing before me
Tempting me to be absorbed
Like a vortex compelling me
Into your embrace.
Feeling your need and
Needing you too,
I am your helpless
Captive for a moment
Then suddenly I compose
And impose my reality,
Escaping your enchantment
Before I am lost again.

Ying and Yang

Oh, he sways to my Yang
While I swing to his Ying,
We call it synchronicity
As I laugh at his jokes
He sighs at my prose
We call it sympathetics
When I massage his feet
Our eyes always meet,
We call it reciprocity.
He keeps bringing me flowers
That blossom for hours,
We call it so nostalgic
So as time and osmosis,
Entwine our emotions,
We call it devotions.

Stuff of Life

The hidden stuff in you reacts
To the hidden stuff in me.
What a wonderful explosion of
Energy is ignited by our essence.
This magnetic flow, unseen,
Unscientific and unexamined
Is the mighty stuff of life
That is expanding, expressing
And escaping into joy in the
Universe without a beginning
And without an end.

The Challenge of Love

To give your heart away
Is such a joyful experience;
Every smile and every hug
Is a silent expression
Coming from your spirit.
It is love in action,
The gift of sharing yourself
Your life, your love, your resources,
And speaks volumes about you.
The light coming from you
Ignites the source in me
Opening me to wonderful magic
That holds you and keeps you
In my heart and memories forever.

Light

I will fill your life
With stars and sun and light
To enliven all our cells and
Increase the adrenalin flow.
I will spark your intellect,
Push your ambitious buttons,
Kiss all the bruised places,
Pat your considerable ego,
Loving you with every breath
Of my existence until
The darkness comes and then
I must leave to join eternity.

Winter Love

We are entwined
In an everlasting dance
Of phoning
Meeting
Talking
Listening
Traveling
Eating
and
Touching
Each others' hearts
With our glances
Questions
Kisses
Embraces
Flowers
Gifts
and
Promises.
No more seeds
Are planted anymore
To water
Germinate
Fertilize
Cultivate
Preserve
Prize
and
Remember
How we loved each other
In the winter of our lives.

Yesterday Before Breakfast

Yesterday before breakfast
He brought me a perfectly
Shaped deep pink rose,
Symbolic of his very
Sensitive open heart.
It spoke eloquently,
Revealing his earnest
Steadfast spirit that
Whispered volumes to me,
Entering my senses
With an exhilarating
Lightness, uniting us
With a force where
Words were superfluous.

Prime Time

In the bright Prime Time
Of my ebbing life
The Apple of My Eye
Has a shiny bald spot
Never ever noticed
When his warm soft hand
Fondly touches mine,
As his ancient songs
Reach my aging heart and
I lose my senile sanity
To our synchronicity.

Memories

Opening my heart to love today,
Remembering your soft gentle voice,
I feel your hand on mine
Your comfort, your arms, your eyes
Come into my memories of you
Warming me with each remembrance.
You kept me steady by your love.
It was in the silent moments together
That I absorbed the essence of you
That brought me joy and gladness
To my open heart and made me yours.
We walked and talked and held each other
For twelve wonderful short years but
You taught me love by simple acts;
You brought bright flowers in your hands
And beautiful jewels with glittering gold
Symbols of your steadfast loving ways
Until one day you left me only
Memories to nourish and sustain me.

Now and Then

Now and then I remember how
I was thrilled by your touch,
Or saw the twinkle in your eye,
Wondering what you were thinking.
I lost myself dreaming about you
Long before I ever met you.
It was in those years of
Wondering and wandering
I lived a kind of fantasy
About how we would know
We were meant to live together
For many years. I just knew
You would love me, honor me
And always be true.
I think I needed you
To find me, to help me grow
In wisdom and patience.
I was always thinking
We would meet sometime
And instantly know
We would be together
For a very long time.
Something was magnetized
In each of us as if
We had known each other
In another lifetime and were

Reconnecting in this time and place
To complete a promise we made
To each other a century ago.
True love lasts forever, they say
Either on this planet or some other.
So now I am dreaming of meeting you
On Venus next time,
Recognizing you again
By the twinkle of your eye.

Photographs

LEFT: Geraldine Patterson (age 19 months), Chicago, Illinois, 1919

CENTER: Geraldine (age 21), father James E. Patterson, mother Rose, sister Shirley (age 17), 1937

BOTTOM: Grandfather John L. Patterson, aunt Irene, grandmother Martha, father James E., uncle John E.

TOP LEFT: Glendale, CA, 1936-37

TOP RIGHT: Association of Aviation Underwriters, 1937

BOTTOM LEFT: With Margaret Hopton, Glendale, CA, 1937

BOTTOM RIGHT: Catalina Island, 1938

TOP LEFT: Bill and Jerri, Santa Monica, CA,
summer 1940

TOP RIGHT: William and Geraldine Mattson,
married December 21, 1940

BOTTOM LEFT: Bill, Jerri, their daughter Marsha,
sister Agda Mattson, father Aligimus Mattson,
Beaverton, OR, summer 1943

ABOVE: With daughters Marsha and
Marilyn, Lake Gregory, CA, September,
1945. William died November 5, 1945.

ABOVE: Marilyn and Marsha Mattson, Easter 1946.

ABOVE RIGHT: George and Geraldine Brillhart, Thanksgiving 1947. They married January 27, 1948

RIGHT: George, with step-daughters Marilyn and Marsha, and daughter Suzanne, 5th Avenue, Los Angeles, CA, Thanksgiving 1950.

TOP LEFT: Jerri with mother Rose Bachman, Marilyn, and Marsha

TOP RIGHT: Suzanne Brillhart

LEFT: Marsha, Jerri, and Marilyn, December 1954

ABOVE: Jerri (age 38), 1955

TOP: Suzanne, Marilyn, and
Marsha, high school portraits

ABOVE LEFT:
Jerri, January, 1960

ABOVE RIGHT:
Mother Rose Bachman

RIGHT:
Jerri, Holland American Line
Carribean cruise, 1978

ABOVE: Jerri and George, 30th wedding anniversary, January, 1978

LEFT: Laguna Beach, CA, Christmas 1988. George died March, 1989.

Photographs on Page 110

ABOVE RIGHT: Jerri and Dick Gerkhe, August, 2001

RIGHT: Jerri reading her poem at daughter Marilyn's 73rd birthday party, Walnut Creek, CA, January 2017

1. Grandson Jason Hanf with wife Lisa | 2. Grandson Mat Hanf with mother Marsha and his partner Mo-Ching | 3. Mat on drums

1. Jason with his son Kyle, father Fred Hanf, son Kasey, and brother Mat at Katelyn's graduation | 2. Marsha with her grandaughter Katelyn Hanf

1. Grandson John Lund with daughter Mira Rose

2. John's daughter Uma and wife Alycia

3. John's mother Marilyn with Mira Rose

TOP LEFT: Suzanne, Marilyn, and Marsha, 1980s

CENTER LEFT: Marilyn, Marsha, Jerri, and Suzanne, 2016

ABOVE: Marilyn and Marsha, Bellingham, WA, 2016

TOP RIGHT: Marsha with husband Michail, 2016

CENTER RIGHT: Jerri's 99th birthday, September, 2016

ABOVE: At home, 2016

112

Meditations & Affirmations

Invocation

Let us go within to that sacred place where we know we are one with the Presence of God. It is at this point of awareness we take our empty cup and allow it to be filled with the blessings of peace, harmony, joy and love that are always available. We are each the beloved, and we are abundantly supplied with everything we need at the time we need it. We go forth this day knowing the presence of God is in our hearts, and so it is.

Sacred Circles

Each of us lives within a connection called a Sacred Circle. We are immersed in this divine perfection of infinite completion. We enjoy the benefits of this great mystery simply by the act of breathing. We are nourished by the *Prana*, the life force, that flows through us with each breath, pulsating through our bloodstream, giving strength to all our cells and tissues, expanding and contracting in a rhythm of natural miracles that keep the moving parts of us repeating the Sacred Circles within.

Renewal

The cross is the symbol of spirituality. As I lift my thoughts vertically, meditating on the miracles surrounding me, I reach out horizontally to communicate, knowing that the bread of life in my basket will nurture and sustain my spirit, as well as furnish others with its wholeness and renewal.

Treasure

The path to your treasure is within. It is always a lifetime journey consisting of hopes of every kind, some were right and some were wrong, while others are puzzles forever. Though the path be long or as brief as a song, it will always lead you home.

Divine Right Action

Today I am filled to overflowing,
Needing only to be here listening
To the still, small voice that
Always tells me how many times
I just need to connect
With the peace within the moment
That furnishes me the truth
Of just being still
And allows divine right action
To take place in me
As every day is holy and happy now.

The Radiance

Today I contact the center
Of radiance in the secret
Mysterious center of myself
Where peace and love
Sustain my life and health,
Rotating all of my cells,
Atoms and breath that keep
My body, mind and spirit
Able to serve and bless everyone
At this time in the universe.

Ever-Present Flow

Let us this day
Dissolve, destroy and delete
All fears and illusions
From our confused minds,
And think only of building
Belonging and bringing
Faith to our everyday lives
As we create, construct and complete
All of our wonderful goals
Filling our lives with
Beauty, balance and blessings
Using constant awareness
Of the ever present flow!

Safe and Secure

I know that I know
There is always a
Safe place within
That is a heaven
Of peace, wisdom
Love and joy
Where I always rest
To balance and listen.
This sacred space
Within my heart
Is all I ever need
To place my body
Soul and spirit
To keep me safe
And secure.

Just for Today

Today I am fully nourished
By the radiant Infinite Light
Filling all my daily needs.
A day at a time I claim joy
That brings me peace and love,
Contentment and much wisdom
To sustain my heart and spirit,
With inspiration from the Infinite.

Heart Song

I become really alive
When I feel so thankful
For my life and its value.
In that space of deep awareness,
I realize that I was never alone.
There was a mysterious aura
That whispered within me,
Giving me ideas to sustain,
Direct and comfort my heart,
Carrying me forward to love,
Forgive and forget all the
Sorrow, old wounds and bruises,
Until my heart and my spirit
Learned to sing, enabling me
To once again join the voices
Of the multitudes that sing
Songs of love, peace and joy.

Infinite Love

The flow of infinite love
Is blessing me today and always
In minute and perfect ways,
Lifting every aspect of my self
Into the reality of peace and joy.
I am in the continuous flow
Of wholeness of mind and spirit.
In this realm of light, I reach up
And beyond into the Infinite
Of divine perfection and am healed
Of uncertainties and false appearances
As I behold only divine love this day.

Harmony

From the highest source
The place of calm assurance
I am united with peace
As the wisdom enfolds me
The feeling soothes my concerns
My spirit now nourishes my body,
Mind and essence, enabling
My eyes to be filled with
Visions of harmony
Lifting and sustaining
All the atoms, cells and molecules
Into a rhythm of perfection,
Supplying every need.

Awareness

Listening to my
Heart beat,
Becoming aware
Of the rhythm
And the sounds
Of the flow of life
Through me, while
Closing all my senses
And going to that
Quiet place within;
I muse on the wonders
Of the Infinite
So vast and beyond
My comprehension.
Likewise, I try and try
To understand
The intricate paths
Of veins and muscles
Skin and bones and organs
That know how
To keep the even beat
And make my brain hum
My voice sing
My eyes glisten
My legs dancing
And my heart rejoicing
All at the same time.
What a wonderful miracle we are!

Tides of Life

Some unseen force of nature flows through the tides of the oceans. This continuous and steadfast action has an infinite purpose, just as our lives reflect and mimic the ebb and flow of the tides.

We are somehow connected to the tides of the earth. We must acknowledge the same rhythm in ourselves so that we can experience balance and live in harmony with the Infinite. Our bodies will be nourished and sustained by just believing we are constantly guided by a Higher Power.

The tides of my life have carried me through all these years and brought me my share of adventures. I am still surviving and exceedingly glad that I am still flowing along.

Heart Space

The heart needs space
To synchronize with Infinity.
The heart needs space to
Tune into unconditional love.
The heart needs space to be
Nurtured by harmonious thoughts.
Stand guard over your heart space
To keep enemies of pain and dis-ease
From entering your Holy Temple.
Open up your heart space
And listen to the Eternal Flow.

Solitude

With outstretched arms
I gather in my lifelong friend
Called Solitude.
So many hours spent together
Pondering life's facets
Wondering why and how
And where we all are going,
Letting unseen forces guide
My thoughts and feelings,
Tossing sometimes in a shiny sea
Of lassitude, while gathering strength
And changing attitudes
That help by giving latitude
To some wise reverent beatitude,
That penetrates the mysteries
Of this lifetime journey.
So many among the multitudes
Are destitute when it comes to
Knowing of the riches
And the lasting gratitude
That can be found
With a close companion
Called Solitude.

Tapestry

The tapestry of our lives
Is woven thread by thread
As thoughts create a pattern
Of every day events.
For in our mind we weave
The scenes of what will be
As castles appear and vanish
In our magical history.
If our life needs more drama
We add some brilliant hues
Taking perfect cues from all
Those lessons we acquired
In another time and space.

Let Me Be

Let me be the vessel
To receive the flow of love
Giving me the strength
To be everything that Thou
Would have me be.
Let me be the heart
That opens with compassion
To understand Thy Will
That seeks to bless and benefit.
Let me bring each closer
To the center of themselves
So each can be Thy servant
By thoughts and words of love.

Coming Home

A dimensional shift of reality
A letting go of mental storage
A lifting to a higher octave
A realization of an inner harmony
A place of rest
A complete relaxation
A cessation of mental chatter
A knowing and being aware
A feeling of arriving
A complete acceptance of self
Like coming home
After being to a foreign country
And the body is weary
But ready to do the will
Of the inner self
Like being born to the perfection
Of all imagination,
An empty cup
That waits to be filled,
A spiritual acceptance
Of tranquility,
A perfect state of rest.

Ten Principles of Abundance

Principle One

The abundance of God's love is displayed throughout the Universe in the beauty of the natural world. Our finite minds cannot begin to comprehend the richness of the universe. We are so magnificent it is difficult for any of us to truly fathom the many wonders with which we are endowed. We are forever expanding, forever moving forward through cycles and rhythms of change.

Principle Two

The source of all my good is that which I AM. The Indwelling Presence prepares my way and provides me with every good in my life. I can never be separated from this all-wise, all-knowing, all-loving Presence that is closer to me than my breath. I am thankful for the abundance that flows through me. I know I am the Beloved.

Principle Three

Abundance is a consciousness of the Inner Presence that desires only joy and prosperity in my life. I let go of any illusions that act as barriers to my prosperity. I allow the divine flow to bring me all forms of love, fulfillment of my creative endeavors, and joyous companionship. I see this Divine Presence manifesting in all my relationships and I am at peace.

Principle Four

My Spirit (my God Self) supplies me with abundance of every kind. I know that everything arrives in my life for my highest good. My breath is part of the life force that feeds my spirit and sustains me always. My feeling nature is nourished by the Divine Presence, which flows through me and blesses me and those around me.

Principle Five

God is the source of unlimited supply and provides me with everything I need now and in the future. It is constantly creating cycles of peace, harmony, love, joy, and wisdom. I rest secure in the infinite possibilities that are unfolding.

Principle Six

The Divine Presence constantly offers experiences that satisfy my heart's desires. Abundance of every kind blesses me and those close to me. My intuition is always available, reminding me that my every need is supplied on time and in time.

Principle Seven

True abundance comes from total surrender to the Divine Will. There is a spiritual struggle fought daily between our lower and higher selves. This is a growth process. My Ego steps aside and acknowledges that my Higher Self be given precedence over the lower self. I am aware of this truth and each day I turn within to communicate with the Divine Spirit. The process of "letting go and letting God" leads to abundance and this is my responsibility.

Principle Eight

Spirit appears in every form and experience, and my cup overflows with miracles. Marvelous creations appear around me and through me and I am immersed, enveloped and surrounded by miracles of love. I speak my Word for the best possible outcome, whatever it may be, and then let it rest, knowing that perfect solutions have already begun to manifest.

Principle Nine

I am always in the flow of Divine Consciousness. This flow is my intuition and imagination, and is always constructive, peaceful, joyous, and abundant. The flow fills me with every good, and I am totally fulfilled. This is the secret and mystery of life. The activity of Divine Abundance is always operating in my life and I am aware of its flow and am thankful.

Principle Ten

Abundance is working as right action in my life. My faith in this principle of abundance leads to right activity in all my affairs, my love relations, my health, my friendships and my finances. I thank God for bringing daily miracles to fruition. I let go of limitations and embrace only the good, the true, and the beautiful.

Motherhood

From my heart and soul I write this to you, my daughters. Mother love is such a mixture of attitudes that blend the many aspects of love. As a mother gives her physical body in an act of love, she brings forth a new life that she nurtures physically, mentally and spiritually. It is a wonderful privilege and awesome responsibility.

Each mother is truly doing the best she can, considering where she is in the cycle of her development. Her problems become the child's problems, and in turn, each child should work through those problems in their own unique way. This process can result in growth and blessings. By choosing their parents, each person has spiritually accepted the gift of life along with the lessons they need for the growth of their soul. Of course, in the final analysis, the only lesson is love.

It is a constant challenge to control the mind and allow growth of the spiritual self to come through. The conflict is always between our higher and lower selves. We may blame everything on the outside world, but eventually we come to realize that we must return to our Father's House, which is our spiritual self.

We must be willing to give up our self-righteousness, and the projection of our faults on others, such as envy, jealousy, hate, resentment, anger, etc. These are all internal conflicts and have no basis in truth. Our mind deceives us through false judgments and perceptions. We hang on to these erroneous beliefs, like treasures in the attic of our minds.

In order to free ourselves from this prison of illusion, we must awaken to our own divine essence. This is the real transformation. With each glimpse of truth about ourselves, we gain a little more understanding and continue to move through cycles of problem solving and growth. We slay one dragon in ourselves at a time. We can never be a victim of anyone or anything unless we do not have the courage to take action to change our position. We remain a victim as long as we are ignorant of our own power.

A mother is there to point the way. The child can benefit from her mother's experience or choose to grow in a different way, which may be entirely unique but necessary for her own transformation. The wise mother allows the space and freedom for the child to walk her own Path of Enlightenment.

To My Daughters, With Love

Within my heart
I held the seed of you
Within my mind
I held the seed of you
Within my soul
I held the seed of you
Until one wonderful day
Each of you just appeared
Crying, laughing, and asking
For the sustenance to
Fill all your various needs.
So very joyously we blended
And bonded every day,
Wondering and learning how
To grow together with love.

To Marilyn

You are my lovely middle daughter.
You are filled with many talents.
Everyday you surprise us all.
Being original and very authentic
Always changing, expanding, growing.
Never giving up, just demonstrating
Your divinity and uniqueness.
You fill my life with so much joy.

The Miracle

For Suzanne

I know who you are.
You are the glow of the moon,
The twinkle of stars,
The sparkle of sunshine.
You are everything that is magic,
A mystery and a miracle,
Living here before me.

Link of Love

For Marsha

Sixty-three years ago
I first held you in my arms.
Before that moment you were
Lying close to my heart
Floating in an inner place
Of a miraculous origin
Finally bursting forth
Through all my agony
Greeting me face to face.
Your love called out to me
In that first meeting.
I cried with thanksgiving
While my hands and heart
Began the caring and sharing.
Quickly passed the years
Feeding, walking and talking
As you learned your ABCs.
Bonding and conditioning
Taught us both the needed
Lessons of ties and memories
While planting seeds that grew,
Linking our past and future.

Here and Now

For Suzanne

I look at you and your essence,
Seeing the magic of this revelation
Speaking to me and sharing this miracle
Of life in this time and place.
I am rejoicing in this wonderful space
Of acceptance coming from your love.
It lightens my path to know that
You are living close to me and
I am enjoying your smile,
Your voice, your heart
Rejoicing with you in
The here and now.

A Trio of Daughters

In my family, music began when I opened my front door one day in the Spring of 1948 while living in Los Angeles. There stood a young man inquiring if I had any children who would be interested in learning to play the violin. My oldest daughter, Marsha, was almost seven years old and I immediately thought of her. He explained that the music school was only about a mile away and that they would furnish a half-size violin to get her started.

Marsha had never expressed any desire to play an instrument but I felt she should be given the opportunity to try. She began lessons and the first song she played over and over again was "Down By the Sea." She was so proud of herself. She brought music to her sisters, who followed by taking piano lessons. The youngest, Suzanne, not only played the piano but developed a beautiful soprano voice. To this day, my daughters perform together at family gatherings, retirement homes, and parties. As a mother, I always just clap my hands!

In 1992, all three daughters remarried within a few weeks of each other. The following poems were written in honor of their weddings.

Marsha and Michail

May the joy and harmony today
Be a light along the path
Of your life together.
May God's love guide you
To enjoy the blessings
That true love creates.
May you always be aware
Of the truth of your
Spiritual essence
Uniting your souls
In wisdom and love.

May 21, 1992

Suzanne and Steve's Dream

We are living proof
Of the inspiration of our dreams.
If void of dreams, we are without
Purpose, goals or commitments.
So this evening we acknowledge and
Congratulate Suzanne and Steve,
Knowing that their marriage is
A realization of their dreams.
May their life together be
Fulfilled with their own dreams of
A union of love, joy and happiness.

May 22, 1992

Marilyn and Dail

May this union be for
Your mutual growth and the
Realization of your dreams.
May your path be illuminated
By a high sense of devotion
To your inner potentials and
Timeless awareness of your
United spiritual strengths.
May you share your virtues and
Communicate your deepest feelings,
So that eternal values will
Sustain your blessed marriage.

June 13, 1992

Change Your Mind,
Change Your Life

The perfection of divine order prevails throughout the universe. We can witness perfect right action in the sunrise and sunset each day. There is an order and rhythm in the seasons. The ocean tides are precise in their action. All creatures, above and below, move with the changes of the earth. Universal laws govern everything. It is humankind's work on earth to obey these laws and to use them to bring happiness. When God's laws are understood and used correctly, then life flows harmoniously.

Along with physical laws, we have spiritual laws to guide us. If we are thankful for the life given to us by God we should be filled with happiness and love. If we always keep our mind on the good, the true, and the beautiful, then our life will automatically be a heaven on earth. To keep our thoughts on joy, we have to work hard to keep out the bad thoughts, which might be hate, anger, resentment, or self-pity. Becoming aware of the hidden thoughts within us can be a lot of heavy thinking!

To be happy, we have to lighten up. We have to eliminate the negative and dark thoughts that can become an obsession. We have to learn what our mind is doing to our body and to our experiences.

As we shift our attention to positive thoughts, we want to sing, dance, draw, write and let ourselves become like children, happy all the time and just enjoying each moment. We get depressed by thinking and rethinking sorrowful thoughts. This kind of darkness in our minds makes us want to do things to forget our thoughts.

Some people start drinking alcohol so they can escape their thoughts. Some people use narcotics to space out so they can't feel anything. Others gain weight because the body wants protection. These people end up in a lot of trouble abusing their bodies when they go against the spiritual laws.

Every moment we choose the kinds of thoughts we let into our mind. It is up to each of us to choose wisely and keep ourselves happy. We can't blame anybody else for what is going on in our head. We can gladden ourselves by what we believe. So do yourself a favor and be good to yourself!

* * *

Do something different every day. If you are in the habit of being miserable and unhappy, change your patterns. You can change your physical patterns and, by doing so, you change your emotional patterns. Start reading things you never read before. Start writing things you never wrote before. If you are bored, you should change your patterns because you are bored with the same old stuff. We stuff our minds with stuff!

Pay attention to your habits. Pay attention to the habits you force other people into. Catch yourself saying, "You always do that," or "You always do it that way." People may put you in categories. Don't be afraid to reach out and be different. You encourage others to be different when they see you being different

We are experts at misery. Don't be afraid to raise a person's consciousness by sharing how you overcame something. Say, "We are all here to learn. We are here to love unconditionally, all things, at all times, in all ways."

How you see yourself you become. A good comment when someone criticizes you is to say, "You might be right. So far I am thinking negative but I am becoming more positive."

* * *

As children, we are like sponges, absorbing the attitudes and beliefs of those around us. We pick up mannerisms, anger and resentment that we hear, observe and mimic. These external stimuli shape our beliefs about ourselves, both in negative and positive ways. These patterns of thinking are molded into our

144

personalities. Our minds and senses are trapped by them. In order to gain some control and explain our actions and attitudes, we see-saw back and forth by either praising or blaming others for why we behave the way we do.

All of this mental maneuvering is because we have not yet reached a state of true discernment. We are not willing or able to sit down with ourselves to discover that we are the culprits, and that we create the drama in our life by our own attitudes and beliefs. To come to self-realization, it is necessary to open our spiritual eyes and be an impartial observer of ourselves, working out a reconstruction program of our own personality, discarding what is causing a short circuit in our behavior.

Now, this is an inside job and can only be done with diligence and patience. As we begin to discard worn out beliefs and attitudes, we will feel lighter and more joyous, and we will change in subtle ways.

* * *

Change of body, mind and spirit takes place at every moment. We are expanding and contracting with every breath. We are enlivened and inspired continuously because we are alive. Parts of us may be replaced, parts may need upkeep, nourishment, inspiration and will power. Some parts have yet to be born. We are part of the Cosmos and our light is always being ignited by a higher source. We are unfolding spirits and eternal life is our birthright.

Writing down my blessings every day is the reminder I need to keep free from any negative memories of the past. In fact, I now look back on past mistakes, regrets or failures as times of learning and growth. Everything is really an opportunity to grow healthier, wiser, kinder, more loving and more compassionate. The only way we learn is by picking ourselves up and trying to be more dependable and loving individuals. We become our own best friend and find happiness within.

As we all know, change is constant. Every day we observe something good and something bad. It is our choice to keep balanced with the faith that brings us peace. The all-knowing voice whispers, "Keep the faith of remembering you are always living in the light that sets you free."

We choose the right way to be and to behold the divine essence within ourselves. This balances, heals, and strengthens our heart to be all we desire to be.

* * *

Changes

We are in a constant state of change. Thank God for change! Stagnation is a curse and creates nothing.

People are always searching outside of themselves, asking for changes to occur in everyone but themselves. They seek help from the government, from religious organizations, from schools, from the health system, from scientists, and from military power. Always outside themselves, to no avail.

We are all witnessing global chaos that brings much havoc, hate, enemies, bloodshed, and mass destruction. All of these disasters are events caused by erroneous beliefs.

It is much easier to blame others for what happens in our lives. It is much more difficult to listen for solutions that come from the Spirit within. We all have choices about what values we will live by. Solutions will come from listening to your own heart.

Each day we have choices about what cause to join or support, what candidate to vote for, what food to put in our body, what clothes we will wear, how we will love our relatives and ourselves, what positive thoughts and beliefs we will harbor, and how we will respond to the guidance of our Spirit.

We must assume responsibility for our own life and attitudes. So let us welcome positive and constructive ideas that will enhance our well-being as we journey along this life of constant change.

Patterns

Our minds can make us happy or sad, depending on our focus. We all have habits of behavior. We each have created patterns of action and reaction to situations, ideas, people, and things.

Sometimes we view others and just know how they will respond to us before they actually do. We have patterns of response to certain situations and always do the same thing over and over.

We can see a certain style or behavior being repeated in our spouses, children, and friends. We observe them and build in our minds a picture of them as being reliable, loving, creative, and intelligent. They may also exhibit negative character traits, such as impatience, intolerance, indulgence, extravagance, or impulsiveness.

We perceive them through our senses and over time they have acted or reacted in certain set patterns. Are the patterns good or bad? Perhaps they are survival techniques developed when they were young, and which served their needs at the time.

We say to ourselves, "That is always the way they act," and we place them in our mind's eye as having a certain kind of personality. As we "see" them, they respond to us in this expected manner. We are expecting this kind of behavior. What we think is what we experience.

It is a known fact that one teacher can bring out the worst in a child, while another teacher can bring out the best. How does this happen?

The pattern of the experience is in the belief of the teacher. If she knows the child can learn, she can find the way to help that child grow and learn. Patterns or habits can be changed, modified or destroyed by a belief. The possibilities of your ideas are the diamonds in your mind.

Focus on Joy

Joy is an emotion I cherish. Joy is also a by-product of love. For by giving and receiving love, I feel joy. If I think about being happy, my body feels better. The joyful thoughts enliven all my cells and energize me.

There were hard times in my life when I used my thoughts and emotions to change directions. I literally talked myself into becoming joyful. Learning to change a negative condition into a positive one has been a wonderful experience.

Seeking more joy, I sometimes use my imagination by writing poetry, which, in turn, sometimes appears in print and may be helpful to others. Another way I use my imagination is to paint watercolor abstracts that give me and others joy. To me, each day is a great experience when I focus on joy.

The Secret

Encourage expression of the spirit
Through listening to yourself.
Encourage the growth of your
Own divine connection.
Encourage simplicity in each moment
By listening to your still, small voice.
Return to this space of stillness
To the real world of wisdom.
Fill yourself from the center
Where the spiritual world exists.
Simplicity is going to the summit
Asking and receiving and giving.
This is the sacred secret of being.

Your Creation

What you think about, you become
What you believe, becomes your life
What you ask for, you receive
What you desire, becomes your reality
What you envision, becomes your experience
What you fear, comes upon you
What you love, you attract to you
What you hate, you give power to.
Choose only what you want to have and be
Because you are the creator of your destiny
Because you grow from your own experiences
Because your talent multiples with use
Because you are the gift in your life
Because you give yourself your own happiness
By the use of the good already within you.
So accent the positive with
Right thinking and right action.
Believe in your own ability
To create your own abundance by
Becoming your own wonderful creation.

Keep Changing

The most important work for me
Is to keep changing myself.
It has been a lifetime pursuit,
Checking on how often the temperature
Of my love is rising each day,
How flexible is my heart in the way
I pray for myself as well as
Those I have never met.
When does my fear need adjusting
To that of faith and truth?
How do I practice forgiveness when
My righteousness is always right?
When do I always love my neighbor?
When does my anger interfere?
A lifetime of reading does not help
An unforgiving heart to change
But continual practice of forgiveness does.

Beloved Infinity

You are a living, working miracle.
You came out of the blue
To express yourself in a unique way.
You are surrounded and immersed in love.
It is this unseen essence that inspires you
To be a witness to the splendor that
Pulsates in each living thing.
It is unseen on this planet.
It is felt and known
Only by your unconscious.
You know in your soul who you are.
You will return to the blue
But you will return
Again and again to Infinity.
You are the Beloved.

Miracles

Let us talk about miracles. Some say they occur through some mysterious power. Parents pray for God's help to save their child's life and a miracle takes place allowing the child to be healed. In a split second, a person averts death and it is called a miracle.

One could say that miracles are happening somewhere every moment of the day. Is there a way to create miracles? The one thing that comes to mind about miracles is that it is necessary to have faith in a supernatural power. When we separate the word "supernatural," we discover that it is *natural*, but of a *super* power. This power is above our five senses. Where does this power come from and how do we claim it for our own use?

It is said we must have hope, faith and trust. How can we trust an unseen force if we do not have faith? If we sat very still and slowed down our doubting minds, we might hear the still, small voice within that gives us an idea. In order to catch this idea, we must have an open mind without skepticism and allow a little faith to inspire a realization about ourselves.

We might ask ourselves how is our breath used by our body to nourish every cell to function and keep us healthy? To me, breathing is a living miracle that even science cannot fully understand. What miraculous system sustains this environment? We might call it a "life force" or a kind of power that holds life together in every form. As we meditate on our breath, we become one with this life force and calm ourselves. We are nourished and supplied by an unseen substance. Think about that. It is the presence of this sustaining power that is our life. Our life is one small miracle.

Multiply this idea by billions of miracles throughout the universe and you begin to understand the vast power that exists.

How can anyone say they don't feel connected or don't have a sense of unity with this power when every moment they are sustained and nurtured by it?

All we need to do is focus on miracles to be able to see them and experience them in our lives. We literally have to surrender our minds to a cosmic way of looking at ourselves and life. Then, we will discover that each day is a joyous and wonderful explosion of diversity and beauty.

This power is only seen with hearts and eyes that understand the meaning of life and its treasures. Those who do not have eyes to see or ears to hear must stay in poverty, chains, pain, resentments, anger and weakness. It is our choice of thoughts that create our state of being and bring miracles to pass.

A Million Miracles

Every day a million
Miracles occur within
The universe of energy.
Life creates changing
Forms of beauty,
Dazzling our five senses
With explosions of
Dynamic sounds, smells,
Sights and synergy
While spinning in
Space systematically!

Approval

Everyone is a unique expression and
A living personification of love,
A perfect manifestation of divine order,
Striving to become more
Of their own perfection.
As the sunflower can only be a sunflower
And a radish can never be a green bean,
So you are a perfect expression of spirit
Forever unfolding, forever discovering
New facets of yourself, flowing
Within the unseen spirit within you.
And believing in your hidden splendor
You reach for the growth found
In your inner sanctuary,
Listening to the still, small voice
That becomes your closest friend
And guides you to your awakening
Of the untapped power that lies
Waiting for you to exercise
Your will and imagination
To mine the diamonds
Of your mind.

Tuning In

Tune into the Infinite
Pick up the heavenly news
Find out how to be happy
In this Age of Thinking Up.
Get with joy and peace
Get with harmony and
With every single beat
To help you sing today.
Walk along life's highway
To meet the golden glow
Streaming in the atmosphere;
Catch a stray sunbeam to
Brighten up your thoughts;
Ride upon a falling leaf
Sailing through the air;
Laugh at drifting clouds
Making pictures in the sky
Helping you smile and love
The way you really are.

Smiles

Find a smile in your heart,
Carry it with you all day long
It will keep you happy and free.
This little spark of love
Is there for you to give away
Bring it out and let it shine
Upon everyone and everything
You see this lovely day.
It will help your aggravations
Melt and disappear just by
Getting in touch with your heart
You can gather smiles everywhere.

Time

Let us think about time and how we use and misuse it. We often have heard that there is only "now" time. What exactly is that all about? We refer to "lost" time and let's take "time out." Or we say "We don't have enough time," or we let "time go by."

Some use time wisely, some kill time. Many take time for granted. As we get older, we say "time flies." When we are children, we say "time drags" or creeps along.

Now time is a given. It is for our use. It is free but sometimes by using it without thought, people end up doing hard time. We sometimes say, "I couldn't think of anything to do with three hours of time while I was waiting for my plane to take off."

What is going on all the time? We use time, we kill time, we make time and we spend time. We all have the same amount of time each day. How we put it to work for us or how we dissipate it, gets down to one word and that is CHOICE.

We have choices in time and we are here in this space, so let's take a good look at ourselves and what we do with time and space. The scientists can give us all kinds of hypotheses about such matters, but what is most important in our own lives is what we do with our own space and time.

It is also a matter of attitude and how we make the right investment of our time that brings success or failure. We have to organize our daily time to make it pay off and bring us dividends.

Since it is our individual choice of interests and our talents that create how we spend our time, this gets back to the word "uniqueness." This is where we must decide to use time to get within ourselves and discover who we are and why we were created at this time in history, and figure out how we can use our time to the best advantage. This separates the adult from the child. It is simply how we perceive ourselves and in what way we can best serve others as well as ourselves. Since time changes all of us, we keep changing what we do with time.

When we are young, we think we have all the time in the world, so we dream a lot of "what ifs." Then along comes another person we spend a lot of time with and we get caught up with trying to merge our time with them, and we lose time in various schemes and dreams. Some are failures and some are successes, but all the time we are using our allotted time without too much worry. We have faith that God will show us the way we should be spending our time.

We create pastimes of thrills and recreation that use up our time, as well as our resources. In the middle of our life, we begin to become aware that time is being spent going nowhere.

We can allow ourselves to travel back in time through imagery or by the use of hypnosis. What do we see when we travel back in time? It seems we see ourselves doing certain things, whether good or bad, or without much thought.

We may see ourselves entangled in other centuries with circumstances that tell us what was going on in those other times. Are we repeating the same mistakes we made in those other times? Some say that by looking back in time we can benefit in the "now" time, and get on with the rest of our life.

What is Time?

We use time, we find time, we take time.
We cannot keep time, bury time or fool time.
It is a continuous flow, a perfect rhythm,
Changing, moving, always going forward.
It never goes back, it never stands still.
It is nothing but a measure for our use.
We all receive a certain amount of time.
We spend it, waste it, and often kill it.
But we will never know its value until
We learn we do not have much of it left.
It is then we try to use it more wisely,
Wondering if we have done the best we could
With the time we were given.
As it slips through our fingers
We begin to understand that
Time is a precious element
We squandered and used
Without thought.

About Time

Time keeps ticking
Time keeps slipping away
Time is only an illusion;
It changes in March
When it springs forward
And falls back in the Fall.
Time waits for no one.
Time is catching up on me.
My time will be over when
God sends me back home.
Maybe I'll say, "God, not yet,
I still have catching up to do
Just writing more poetry."
God will probably say,
"Well, I'll send you back and
Give you another home
With more time to waste or kill
Or just amuse yourself
On your own time."

Victory

Nothing is ever lost,
It just seems so to our senses.
The autumn leaves of glory
Linger forever in our hearts.
The once held loved one
Lives in a different dimension
That we communicate with
In the quiet peaceful moments.
We say they have died, yet
This is just a necessary change
For time keeps on recycling us
To experience at long last
The victory called Eternity.

This Moment

I live in this moment.
Each moment is all I ever need.
The present moment is all mine,
I use this moment only momentarily.
My real needs are very few.
All I have to remember now
Is to take a breath and inhale,
Then exhale and really know
I am living, active and well.
No need to begin thinking about
My past history, my lost hopes
My lost chances or lost desires.
I am here breathing and alive,
Laughing, and ready to enjoy life.

Today

Awaken to the wonders of today
To the precision of earth's movement
As it rolls along its path
Bringing changes every moment,
Gradually creating seasons
In each and every hemisphere.
Listen to the winds that blow
Across the earth in syncopation
To a higher rhythm that balances
The planets, stars, sun and moon,
Giving us such cosmic benefits.
Today is certain and it is now,
So take this day and use it,
Make it sing and bring you joy,
Squeeze the juices of today
From sunrise to sunset,
Giving you time for loving
Every moment of today's unfolding.

Aging

Age is an attitude, not a length of time. While we are young our attitude is wonder and curiosity. We desire to know what our world has to teach us. After testing our strengths and talents, we move into a larger world, looking for satisfaction and recognition through academic and professional pursuits.

Then, as we try to expand our hearts with loving, it is there we might make some mistakes, pitting our wills and desires against others, trying to hold and master them with our need for companionship. We act out a sort of expected conformity by reading rules in ancient wisdoms, attending sermons in the myriad temples of our universe, or joining forces with a certain clan.

As we age and accumulate experience, we soon discover we will never grow old as long as our hearts are flowing with love, patience, and understanding. Unfortunately, many of us allow age to set in and wrinkle us with things like hate, resentment, fear, anger and ideas that are rigid with self-righteousness.

We must keep returning to that childlike state that reaches toward the new with zestful curiosity and continued learning. Let nature be our teacher as it shows us its renewal every spring, bringing forth eternal harmony and filling our souls with wonder.

Where am I headed? At this stage and age of my life, I am living in the "now." I live a simple life. When I am hungry I eat. When I am tired I sleep. When I swim, walk and talk, I experience my body. When I write, paint and listen to music, my feelings feed my soul. I follow my intuition. As I listen to my intuition, my spirit and soul give me direction.

In my Golden Years, I am just enjoying life. I am just being. I am happy, healthy, peaceful, and evolving every minute. Every day holds laughter, love, joy and inspiration. When my soul is ready to depart, I will be prepared to take leave of my body.

Age is Only A Number

I am ninety going on thirty.
Time is now my friend,
Sending so many new miracles
Into my sphere of awareness,
Opening up my spiritual eyes,
Letting me be divinely aroused
To understand more and more.
Feeding my soul with such joy,
Making my heart sing with
The moon and the stars,
Pushing me on to one hundred
When I shall be going on twenty.

Wisdom

I am now ninety-seven years and
I know the truth of my being.
It is still an ongoing process that
Proceeds according to my faith and belief.
This Power and Presence is everlasting.
This understanding within is forever.
It is always available for my use.
I lift up my eyes and heart just
Allowing this awareness to manifest in
Divine right action today and forever.

Good Will

I have forgotten my past.
It has no validity today.
I can never again relive it;
It is over, used up and forgiven,
Forever and ever disappearing
Without remorse or regret.
Today is bright, alive, ready and
Willing to be used by me to
Bring peace, love and harmony
Filling me with joy and good will.

Unessentials

I am an old lady,
Sometimes forgetting.
But youth also lapses,
Forgetting the mundane.
Aging folks may have
A few slipped clogs
From lack of exercise.
Youth, always on the run,
Leave too much to chance,
Giving up their responsibilities.
Perhaps Youth should borrow
The Old Ager's techniques of
Forgetting the unessentials
Of modern materialistic
Endeavors and open their hearts
To the reality of seeing
The stars, the moon and
The sun that only wisdom
Brings to the present moment.

Why I'm Still Here

It seems to me that the older I get, my life is filled more with keeping myself fit, fed and fancy-free. I am hemmed in on all sides with self-care!

In the past, I took my body for granted and never thought about what food I put in my mouth, but the older I get the more restrictions apply. If I strain too much in one direction, I get a pain here or a hitch there, needing more people to hold me together, like dentists, doctors, nurses, therapists, nutritionists, masseuses, reflexologists, chiropractors, herbalists, exercise analysts, not to mention optometrists, psychiatrists, gurus, priests, ministers, psychics and clairvoyants to peek into my final departure. So many authorities that serve the body, mind and soul! And from time to time, all of us have attended seminars and workshops just to allay our fears and help our dreams come true.

While it takes all of the above service providers to keep me on my journey, I must carry on with all my strength because there still are things to learn and people I must meet whom I may help somehow, somewhere, *because that is really why I'm here.*

If I had been told in advance what the road ahead would be like, I would have said, "No, thanks. I'll just let it pass this time around." Of course, there were moments during my life I would not have changed at all, but when I recall the buckets of tears and heartaches . . . you can have them all!

Most of us spend much more time looking back with regret, remorse, or longing, rather than living in the moment. Taking time to really see what we are experiencing in the "now." The miracle of breathing in and breathing out. The precious inhalation that gives our bodies and minds the fuel to just "be."

A lot of us are so restless, looking forward with such hope and fear, that we let today pass by without savoring its juices. We're always looking at our watches to be ready for the next appointment. Living on "fast forward" instead of idling in neutral by smelling the roses, seeing the stars, and feeling the sunshine as we watch blooms unfold.

As we look into each other's faces and see the sparkle in each eye, what is going on between the exchange of magic and awareness? When a loved one smiles, do we really see their heart or just take it all for granted because they have always been there for us?

Putting everything into perspective, our losses and our gains, can we truly say we moved an inch or two while on this earthly journey? A gain in perception or attitude is an unseen force and only when the heart cooperates with time and change, do we come to realize our worth.

Being Alive

The secret of longevity
Is just a deep sense of peace
That comes from an inner strength,
A true wisdom that you are always
Living, breathing, and being
In the Presence of God's love,
The acceptance of your true Self
That continually nurtures your needs
Of body, mind and spirit,
From everlasting to everlasting.
It is the wholeness of love,
The wisdom of peace and
The joy of just being alive.

When I Am An Old Woman

When I am an old woman
I shall enjoy the
Morning dew at sunrise
If I can be persuaded
To get out of bed!
I shall dance
At someone's party
If they are gracious enough
To invite me!
I shall converse
With young people
Being open to new ideas
If they too will listen
To my pearls of wisdom,
Knowing we need each
Other's exchanges
To keep balanced
As we proceed on
Our journey in life.

Waiting

I have waited for this
And waited for that
Like going to school
Like falling in love
Like getting a job
Like getting married
Like having a baby
Like having one more
Like waiting for grandchildren
Like again and again
Like waiting for wars
To begin or end
Like waiting for fear
To be over and done
Like wanting you close
When you are long gone
Like wanting to leave
For a faraway place
Like wanting to wait
When God says
It's over!

Returning

Let us take time to
Mellow and age
Like a fine wine that
Comes to its peak
Of aroma and flavor
And unique bouquet.
Take time to be quiet
And listen to a voice within
That stills all fears,
Telling us with passing years
More ease is found
With rest we earned.
How memories nourish us
As we move along in years,
Realizing that all illusions,
Agonies and fears
Have vanished
And petty blaming,
Those numerous lies
Made by our lower self,
Brought dis-ease and despair.
But now, in quiet reverie
We contemplate
Our own foolishness,
Moving strongly inward
Until we rest
And know that all
Was for our growth
Making us obedient
To our Higher Self
Returning fully aged
To our soul.

Divine Departure

When I take my divine departure
Let me be ready with a smile.
I will want to leave this earth
With a thought of thankfulness,
Grateful for my many blessings.
With a slight whisper of regret,
Waving farewell to loved ones
Who brightened up my stay,
Knowing we will all meet again
Some way, some how, some day.
Moving into the next dimension
With joyful expectations of
Further joys and changes that
My soul will take me on.
Though the door closes on Earth,
I will greet my real home
As the door opens and
I return once more
And we are united
On the eternal shore

Appendix -
Letters From
Family & Friends

Poetry in Motion

What can be said about a beautiful, vivacious woman who has been riding on the "Big Blue Marble" called Earth for nearly 100 years? Well, if I were to use all the words that ever traversed the marquee in the mind of Jerri Brillhart, the pages filled would be monumental.

Jerri is a soul that magnetically attracts everything good in her path. She's much too busy moving forward in a wondrously engaging manner to be mired by the trivial negativities that hold so many of us back from prosperity.

Immersed in a constant flow of grace with patience awaiting her advance, Jerri's life is sheer poetry in motion. As easily as she breathes, she plucks words from the universal archives and mirrors them back for all to see.

If troubled humans could as easily use words to communicate and understand as she does, so much more beauty would be pushed into form.

I have observed this "Guardian of Words" in action long enough to take with me a life lesson or two. When people banter in lively discussions about the mysteries of the great beyond, I watch as she sits in silence as though she were watching small children trying to play a game of tennis and get one over the net.

After a time of others rallying ideas back and forth, someone will turn to her and ask, "What do you think it's all about, Jerri?" She waves her hand over her head like water on a duck's back, and responds with an "Ehhh." This one utterance says it all. Jerri, thank you for the life you share with us all.

Your friend and admirer,
Gregory Barnes

The Legendary Jerri Brillhart

Jerri Brillhart makes her own legend as she goes along just by being the force of nature that she is. She cannot help just spinning off greatness. She was born with it, and shares it freely. Of course, education helped. Her innate intelligence made a good foundation. And creativity shaped her life, her creativity put to good use through children and family and a lifetime of poetry.

Gloria and I met Jerri when we were invited to attend her 93rd birthday party. We had known Marsha when we all attended a church in Concord. Gloria and I stopped going to that church and were living in Summerset 4. I think Marsha came by Gloria's booth where she was displaying her jewelry at a boutique show. We talked and Marsha invited us to come to her mother's birthday party.

Jerri was warm and welcoming and entirely enchanting. We told Marsha that we were looking for a spiritually uplifting church, preferably in Brentwood. Marsha told us that Jerri attended the Unity Church here and we might like it. We did and we fell in love with Jerri.

Somehow it came out that I am a writer and Jerri invited us to attend a poetry group she was putting together, meeting at her house. Jerri released me from a fear of poetry. She told me that poetry did not necessarily have to rhyme. What a blessing. Jerri and I go and contribute to a poetry group meeting in Brentwood. I am so grateful to her because she has mentored me in this unfoldment of my craft.

Anyway, I guess Gloria and I were supposed to be on the tangential path with Jerri. She has given us the precious gift of love and grace. We treasure it and we treasure her.

Dr. Rev. Leslie Harold

A Birthday Tribute
To My 99-Year Old Mother

As Jerri Brillhart's middle daughter, Marilyn, this is my personal story of what it has been like to be guided and influenced by this living legend. Mother has taught me, by example, how to live life maintaining a balance of body, mind, and spirit. I recalled she followed Gaylord Hauser's health advice. She made yogurt, canned fruits and vegetables, and used a pressure cooker. I remember the weekly groceries for our family of five came to $20 in the 1950s. She was moneywise, thrifty, and she saved money. Dad earned $700 a month. Credit cards were unheard of in those days. I babysat for 50 cents an hour to buy material to make many of my clothes. Later, I worked my way through college, with no loans!

She fostered a healthy lifestyle -- cooking nutritious meals, walking, swimming, and working out, which she continues to do even at the age of 99. On a humorous note, she experimented on us with Sleep Teaching records played from speakers on our bed headboard.

Our home was without a television until I was 10 years old. We played board games and card games. All three of us daughters played music. An expert seamstress, Mom made matching dresses for my sister Marsha and I in our younger years. I fondly recall her sewing my white linen high school graduation dress and satin wedding gown. Mom always made an effort to look her best and take pride in her appearance. She still loves to dress up for social engagements and poetry readings.

We followed Jack LaLanne's fitness classes on TV, doing jumping jacks in the living room. He was our health guru. "I Love Lucy" was our favorite TV show. We laughed ourselves silly!

Summer days on the beach were such fun in Long Beach. I was kept busy doing my share of chores, hanging up clothes, ironing, washing dishes, mowing lawns, and washing the family car. I asked to be the cook in the family at age 11. The artist in me required herbs and spices.

As a spiritual teacher, mother shone as our Religious Science church youth director. She also became a prayer practitioner/chaplain, a role she continues to play at Unity of Brentwood to this day. As a child, she took me to sermons by Ernest C. Holmes, founder of the Religious Science Church. We also attended Manly P. Hall's talks at the Philosophical Research Society in Los Angeles. I was profoundly affected by this early exposure to great philosophers and spiritual leaders.

Most importantly, she is a gifted metaphysical, spiritual poet whose poems have been published in eight anthologies. Some of her great strengths are her positive, youthful attitude and loving, caring compassion for others.

Mom has been my mentor in many areas of my life. After my father died when I was one and a half years old, she showed strength and resourcefulness in earning money by creating a boarding house for women. She taught me how to sew at the age of eight. I took that passion for sewing and fashion, and turned it into my first career. I graduated from UCLA in fashion design and worked as a junior sportswear designer for six Los Angeles manufacturers. At the age of 37, I became an Ordained Minister with the Universal Life Alliance of Santa Monica. Today, my spiritual work is focused on my massage therapy practice, attending to a wide cross-section of people and conditions to treat. Mom, like myself, after retiring from her corporate job, became focused on health work. She offers her specialty, reflexology, to friends and relatives even today. Like her, I love to write and plan to write books.

Mom is a truly remarkable person and spiritual coach. Spending time in her presence is a true gift to anyone she meets. Even when meeting a stranger, she tunes right into them and shares her wisdom and spiritual insights. As with her poetry, she has a direct channel to the source, call it God or a higher power. She is surely a living legend, pure love in action, her inner light shines brightly. She is ageless and timeless.

Mother, I love you.

Your daughter,
Marilyn

To My Mother on Mother's Day, 2002

(This poem was a take-off from a third grader's assignment and art project)

I am so grateful to have you as my Mom!

I wonder how God chose the two of us to meet?

I hear your voice with Spirit calming me down.

I want you to enjoy every moment you have on this earth.

I am that I AM

I pretend we are laughing together at the Marianist Center.

I feel your encouragement to try meditating daily.

I touch your old heart necklace and recall your elegant ways.

I worry when you take so many ambitious trips.

I cry when I forget my best friend, God, is near as my breath.

I AM, I AM.

I understand more as I travel my life's journey.

I say more on my mind than I dared to do long ago.

I dream of what more is in store for all of us in the years ahead.

I try to learn how to compute, and keep up with healthy practices.

I hope my grandchildren will have an easier time than their parents.

I AM that I AM.

From First Daughter, Marsha Joy

Dear Jerri

I miss:
Our friendship
Our writing club
Your enthusiasm
Your laughter
Your hugs
Your stories
Your openness to everyone
Your forgetfulness for slights
Your presence at CLE
Your yeses
Your dancing with life.
No where have I seen you duplicated
So many wonderful qualities in one person.
Your sensitivity
Your intuition
Your practicality.
               I love you, Jerri!
I admire:
Your forgivingness
Your kindnesses
Your fearlessness
Your interest in the world
Your spirituality
Your sharing
Your advice
Your massages.

Your love has brought a smile
to every cell of so many bodies.

Love, Ellen

Dear Jerri

I have many happy memories of our times together during the last 60 years. You have had a profound influence on my life, although you might not realize it.

If you hadn't arranged for me to take your place while you went to Chicago on vacation in 1937, I might never have come to California, wouldn't have met the man I married, nor had the children and granddaughter I have!

You were a role model to follow during the time we shared an apartment. You managed to keep within our food budget; you always did your share of the work; you were reliable in every way. Whenever you received a raise in salary, you used it for something special. You budgeted your finances wisely so that you were able to dress well and take interesting vacations.

Whenever we took vacations together I relied upon you to do any navigating to get onto the right train (in London), to figure out the money exchange, and to make important decisions.

When my back went out after our first night in Amsterdam on a 30-day trip through Germany, Switzerland, and Austria, you provided reflexology treatments twice a day. Without those treatments, I wouldn't have been able to continue on that memorable trip!

You have influenced me in a myriad of ways, Jerri, and I am certain you have done as much for others you have met along the way. May you continue to stay young, healthy, and optimistic, to write poetry, to enjoy life, and to make others happy for years to come!

With love and gratitude,
Margaret

To Jerri on Her 80th Birthday

80th Birthday???!!! That doesn't seem possible. There you are square dancing circles around us, swimming laps past us, "out-exercising" us at the health club. And how about your creative talents? Poetry, painting, writing? Now, shall we mention your skill at bridge and shorthand or your extraordinary willingness to try to help and understand your family and friends? This is well known to all of us. Haven't we benefited from your healing reflexology treatments? Even your enthusiasm for life in general overwhelms us. Your energy amazes us and we wonder how your fellow Elder Hostel travelers keep up with you! When you met and married my father, I felt I finally had a role model at a time in my life when I really needed one. You were a happy woman, raising three daughters, loving my father, cooking up a storm. What an inspiration! Who cares if I gained eight pounds that first year? I was so happy! The truth is, I have learned a lot from you. So, from far away, but straight from the heart, have a wonderful Happy Birthday!

Your step-daughter, Dana
September, 1997

About My Mom

With spiritual awareness from the other side, I chose my birth Mother for this incarnation and I chose well. We have had a few challenges in our sixty-eight year relationship especially in the early years but she has always been on my side. She has been one of my spiritual teachers and my best friend.

Over the last eight years we have been sharing a single family home in an over 55 community called Summerset. When I broached her about moving north and buying a house together after my second divorce, she called me the next day after mulling it over and said, "I put my condo on the market today." She had lived there for 36 years and at 92 was ready to move closer to all her daughters. This woman does not let grass grow under her feet.

I still work full-time and am gone a good deal from home. You therefore must not believe her when she says that "I am her Mother." She loves asking anyone she meets how old they think she is and their answers range from mid-seventies to mid-eighties. They are shocked when she tells them her chronological age and ask for her secrets. One thing she likes to say is, "I keep breathing." But this is my take on it -- she has a positive attitude and sees the lesson in any challenge, she is calm and balanced, she is involved with people and activities that she enjoys, she still exercises at the gym and swims in the summer, she takes many vitamin supplements and has regular chiropractic adjustments.

We have taken several trips together and she is a good traveler, fun to be with and rarely complains. We took two Road Scholar trips. The first in 2011 to Branson, Missouri for a week of musical entertainment and the second to Fort Worth for the finals of the Van Cliburn piano competition in 2013. In 2015 we took a bus trip to Southern California sponsored by Summerset. It was a little more challenging because the steps into the bus were high but we had enough free time to reconnect with several of her friends. There have been a number road trips in between as well, where my sister, Marsha joined us. In October 2016 we spent a weekend in Sonora visiting with relatives. All three of her daughters went on that trip. I point this out to give you an idea of her intrepid spirit and her willingness to stay engaged in life.

Years before we moved in together I knew that when the time was right we would be sharing space. There were many years when we lived in two parts of California and with our busy lives only spent a few days together, at most twice a year. I am making up for that lost time and thoroughly enjoying our relationship and living arrangements.

With all my Love,
Suzanne

CPSIA information can be obtained
at www.ICGtesting.com
Printed in the USA
FSOW02n1037191117
41403FS